Judo Champion

Karen Briggs

Judo Champion

with Nicolas Soames

The Crowood Press

First published in 1988 by
The Crowood Press
Ramsbury, Marlborough,
Wiltshire SN8 2HE

British Library Cataloguing in Publication Data

Briggs, Karen
Judo champion.
1. Briggs, Karen 2. Martial artists – Great Britain – Biography
I. Title
796.8′152′0924 GV1113.B7/

ISBN 1 85223 103 3

Picture Credits

Photograph on page 60 by Phil Brown;
photograph on page 70 by *The Times*.
All action photographs by David Finch.

Dedicated to my parents, Albert and Elsie, who gave me every opportunity to fulfil my sporting career and who, although faced with difficulty at times, would sacrifice their own needs and time to help me achieve success.
Many thanks for your support Mum and Dad.

Typeset by Avonset, Midsomer Norton, Bath.
Printed in Great Britain by
Redwood Burn, Trowbridge

Contents

Introduction

Even after more than twenty years of involvement in the Olympic sports movement, judo is still regarded by the wider public as a form of oriental self-defence. The popular newspapers always go to town whenever there is a suggestion that a 'judo expert' has somehow dispatched a would-be mugger by throwing him hard on his back or strangling him unconscious. A couple of years ago, there was a story of a young schoolgirl who had taken a few judo lessons and, when attacked by a man in the street, threw him and broke his collar-bone.

Stories like these fuel the popular imagination, but most are fabricated to the point of science fiction. It is not that such an incident is impossible – just that it is unlikely. I regard myself as being fortunate in never having been forced to discover whether judo would work in an extreme situation. I am pretty sure that I would take the age-old option of using my fitness and seize the first opportunity of running from any trouble that may start. In fact, this is a time-honoured judo response to trouble. When Jigoro Kano founded his Kodokan Judo in 1882, he determined to ensure that his judo would not be cast in the same mould as many of the ju-jitsu schools which had become the preserve of glorified thugs. So, he forbade all his pupils to get into fights and use judo in the street, no matter how unpleasant the taunts from rivals. In difficult circumstances, Kano ordered, his pupils had to run away from trouble – and they did, for anyone caught fighting back would be summarily dismissed from the Kodokan.

In fact, the effectiveness of judo was proved by a series of formal contests held against the older ju-jitsu schools in those first decades, and by some rather more informal events in the back streets of Yokohama Harbour and other not so salubrious quarters, despite Kano's instruction.

It is this view of judo as combat, rather than the ability to evade trouble at all costs, that has prevailed as judo spread rapidly around the world. I can see it in the eyes of people I meet who do not do judo. I am introduced as the three-times World Champion, and they can't believe how small I am. Even when I explain that judo is a modern sport where contests are held in weight categories and men and women compete separately, as in athletics, I see men thinking: 'How does a tiny girl like that do it . . . there must be some secret,' and the popular misconception of the 'secret art' of judo is fuelled once again.

But children understand. I like doing judo with children – when I am not preparing for a competition. Children generally have a very fresh and open attitude towards judo. First of all, judo is great fun. It is fun to roll around the mat, to throw your friends all over the place, and even to be thrown. At the very early stage they don't think about winning and losing, and it is not very different from a game. Of course, sometimes when I visit a club or a school for the first time, and they see me walk on to the mat with a black belt, they can be terrified – but it never really lasts long. Judo at that level has little to do with self-defence or combat – it is just another sport like football or swimming.

MY LIFE

The 1986 World Championships in Maastricht – attempting to turn Fumiko Ezaki of Japan in the final.

1 School Years

Just another sport – that was more or less how I first saw judo. I started at the age of 11 when I was sport-crazy. I did almost every one I could – whenever I had a spare second, I would be out in the fields running or kicking a ball around. From an early age I seemed to have a great reservoir of energy that had to be expended at every opportunity. Just sitting around drove me mad, and I think I was immensely fortunate to have a family who actively encouraged all my activities, rather than stifled them with platitudes about doing too much, or acting the tomboy.

But it couldn't have been easy for my parents. I am the fifth child of a family of six. My father, Albert, and my mother, Elsie, had their first son, Michael, in 1952, and three other children followed at almost yearly intervals. Philip, Kevin and Anita. I was born four years after Anita, on 11 April 1963, and even my parents admit I was a 'mistake' . . . they had intended to stop at four children. Paul, who was born the following year, was another mistake.

My father was a foreman stevedore on the Hull Docks – which were then far busier than they are now. We lived in a small three-bedroomed house in Abbey Street, Hull which looked out on to the railway line which served the docks. From 5 p.m. to 10 p.m. trains loaded with timber would work their way past our house from the docks to the marshalling yards. All that has changed now, and the railway line has been turned into a housing development.

Family life was busy but warm and friendly. All my older brothers did sport of one kind or another: Michael represented Yorkshire in the triple jump and cross country, Philip played football and Kevin even had trials for Hull City Football Club boys' side. Anita followed a more feminine route – she went to ballet. I tried it, but it was quite clear from the start that it was not for me.

I was always an over-active child. At nine months I was walking and jumping off tables, and I had to be tied in the pram so that I wouldn't get out. Nevertheless, I was always small for my age.

By the time I entered junior school it was becoming very evident that I was an out-and-out tomboy. By this time we had moved from Abbey Street to the new Bransholme estate, built on an old aerodrome. We had a five-bedroomed house – and we needed the extra room – on the edge of the estate looking on to fields. At the time, of course, I had no idea how well I would get to know those fields and how many hours I would spend in them, first of all just playing, and then working at the more serious business of fitness training for judo. In those early years at Bransholme, which grew quickly to become known as the largest housing estate in Europe, I remember spending most of my time playing football with the boys,

At home in Abbey Street with my brothers and sister in 1967: (back, left to right) Philip, Mike and Kevin; (front, left to right) Paul, Anita and me, aged four.

including Andrew Benson, my best friend for many years, or taking on dares to prove that I was every bit as good as they were. I was always the one to go up the tree when the ball got stuck, or climb down into the open drain.

The first competition I can remember was a race in the Beacholme Holiday Camp when I was five. I had been entered in the under-sevens, but when my mother saw the size of the children I was supposed to run against, she said: 'You're not letting her run in that race with them.' I was a bit confused myself, and when all the others set off, I was still standing on the starting line. But one of my brothers gave me a push and I managed to overtake them and win. I suppose that was the first real indication that I had some sports potential.

I was always ready to have a go at anything – except swimming. I created a scene when my father took me to the local baths to teach me to swim, but with great common sense, he didn't force me. He seemed to know that I would come to it in my own time, and I did. When I found that we were going to have lessons in school, I asked him to take me to the baths beforehand to teach me, which he did.

As my time at Kinloss Junior School came to an end and I moved to Bransholme High School, I was doing every sport I could: running, swimming, trampolining, basketball, hockey, rounders and diving; but football was my favourite. I knew all the football teams, their positions in the league, and, despite having Hull City on my doorstep, supported Leeds because they were a First Division side. I would come rushing in from school and within seconds would have changed into shorts and a T-shirt and run outside with a ball. Because we were a large family, with different ages and interests, we all ate at different times. I seemed to live on hastily grabbed meals of baked beans, bread and butter, which took the least time, so that I could be out in the fields or knocking a ball up against the wall. For hours and hours I would practise tap the ball – keeping the ball up in the air with just my thighs, feet and head. I used to drag my father outside to get him to count how many I could do without once dropping it. And, quite by chance, it was this practice that was to put me, at the age of 12, on television for the first time.

Beginning Judo

It was in my last year at Kinloss Junior that I started judo. It was March 1974 and although I was nearly 11, I weighed just over four stone and probably looked around eight. There was a write-up on judo in the local paper; I thought I would like to have a go at it, so my father took me to a judo club run by the National Dock Labour Board. It was held in the building originally used as the call stand – the place where the dockers would gather in the morning to be allocated work. But it was now used for judo and karate, with an old canvas cover stretched over foam rubber mats and tied around a wooden frame at the sides. Although I didn't know it at the time, it was an Amateur Judo Association club, one of the smaller judo organisations that are separate from the main Olympic body, the British Judo Association.

I don't remember much from those first few visits, except that I enjoyed it from the start. I did loads and loads of rolling breakfalls – if I remember accurately, that is all I did in those first lessons – and to me it seemed more like gymnastics than anything else. Only later did I start on the throws, but it was even longer before I started fighting – which, in retrospect, was what I really enjoyed. The class was very strict. We seemed to spend most of the time practising throws, turning in for *morote-seoi-nage*, and doing throw for throw. We learned some holds, but we hardly seemed to do any groundwork at all. *Morote-seoi-nage* became my favourite throw very quickly.

We didn't do very much randori either. For 15 minutes at the end of the class we would be split into two teams, sit on the edge of the mat, and wait for our turn to come out and have a contest. It seemed to me that I waited for hours for my turn, would come out and throw very quickly with *morote-seoi-nage*, and would then have to go and sit down for a long time again which was really boring. I preferred fighting the boys to the girls – it would then be a good fight. Half the time, I think the instructors thought I was a little boy!

The main difficulty I had was the Japanese names. We were supposed to learn all the rolling breakfalls, throws and holds in Japanese; I never seemed to be able to get the hang of them.

For the first few lessons, I went in shorts and a T-shirt, but then, when it was obvious I was going to stick at it, my father bought me a second-hand judo suit for £1.50 from someone in the club. My second judogi, some time later, was also second-hand – from the local paper. But after that I began to get new suits.

One of the instructors, Ray Woods, told my father quite early on that I was a natural at judo, but it didn't mean much because I was good at all sports. I certainly didn't think it was going to be the most important sport of all. I knew that I preferred judo to the karate which went on at the other side of the room. Karate seemed to me to involve people just kicking their legs, punching the air, and making a lot of noise – it didn't appeal to me then, and doesn't now.

I simply enjoyed getting hold of other children and fighting with them, and I didn't care whether they were boys or girls, or how big they were, which was rather unusual for a girl, at least in that club. I had my first grading on 19 May 1974, and was awarded three orange tags, but by the end of the year I was promoted to one green tag.

By this time, my competitive urge had already taken me into club competitions. By good fortune, the National Dock Labour Board judo club in Hull was fast becoming one of the top junior clubs in the AJA, and within a year of my joining we were travelling around the country, kitted out in neat green and orange team tracksuits, taking part in numerous competitions. In my first year I won two gold medals for club events in my weight (around 30 kilos) and in the weight category above, which you were allowed to enter.

In 1975 I entered every judo competition I could get to. I won the AJA Area Championships for under 30 kilos, two weight categories – under 30 kilos and under 35 kilos – in my club championships, and finally the AJA National Championships in Haden Hill, Birmingham, in the under 30 kilos category.

The pattern of the fights was very much the same. I was like a terrier. I would come out fast, take hold of my opponent and run around the mat before shooting in for a *morote-seoi-nage*, which was done standing. We didn't do *drop morote-seoi-nage* because it wasn't regarded as good traditional judo, and even now I have difficulty doing it in contest, although I have very different views about 'drop' techniques. But the competitions were much easier – there was a great emphasis, even at national level, on good style and spectacular throws. It was remarkably difficult to get an ippon for a throw – you virtually had to catapult your opponent to the ceiling, control her all the way down and then land her flat on her back to get the magical maximum score. And groundwork was almost non-existent. If you won on the ground, you almost felt like apologising: 'Yes, I got five ippons, but only one of them was with a throw.'

Which Sport?

Nevertheless, despite this success, football remained my favourite sport. By the age of 12 I was taking football extremely seriously. I became a member of the top women's team in the area, the Hull Brewery, although I still looked only an eight-year-old. I played right wing – my favoured position in all team games, from football to hockey – and my primary ambition at the time was to get into the England women's side rather than to bid for international honours on the judo mat. When I look back, I find it a little strange that I was so happy in a team game like football, when, most of the time, judo is such a solitary event. But I loved travelling to games with the team, and the sense of team play on the football pitch.

I was also fascinated by ball control. I never seemed to tire of the challenge of keeping the ball in the air for hour after hour. As I turned 12, I found I was practising every day for between two and four hours. I imagine that many parents would have regarded it as a complete waste of time, but my parents never complained that I should be doing school work – I always did my homework in any case. And, quite unconsciously, I was learning numerous lessons about training that were to play a vital role in my development as a judo competitor.

For a start, I was learning to concentrate. I used to reach between 1,500 and 2,000 taps of the ball without dropping it quite frequently, and that takes about 90 minutes without a pause. Tap the ball taught me to enjoy training for what it was, and not always to look for tangible results, with the

The football fanatic.

inevitable disappointment when the results are not attained. It taught me to train alone and that my greatest competitor was myself – I had to conquer fatigue, bad technique, and learn to cope with outside forces such as going with the wind when it blows. And I learned crucial lessons about balance, reactions, stamina, and fluency of movement.

It was sheer chance that this led to my first television spot. The father of a boy from a local football club organised a tap the ball competition – partly, I think, in the hope that he would win. About 200 boys entered the competition, but I didn't know about it until a neighbour, Mrs Kathy Dillon, who had seen me practising for hours in the field, told me she had entered me for it. I was the only girl but, frankly, it was no contest. On the day of the competition, the son of the organiser managed the best score of all the boys – 272 – but I kept going, using my feet, knees, thighs, and occasionally my head, until I reached 1,439. Some of the boys said that they could do 700 in practice, but under competition conditions they couldn't keep it up. However, I found that that kind of stress didn't affect me.

The prize was supposed to be a trial with Hull City, but that was obviously not possible, so I was given a £30 cheque instead. It was presented to me at the Hull City football ground by the manager, John Kaye, and I was persuaded to demonstrate tap the ball wearing a blouse and skirt for the press – television and national and local papers, from *The Sun* to the *Yorkshire Post*. Only one observant photographer caught me in a particularly high kick and saw that underneath my feminine clothes was the football kit – Leeds United colours, of course – that I had got as a Christmas present, and that I wore most of the time.

From that first publicity event came displays on television shows, at holiday camps and bingo halls that prepared me, to some extent, for what was to come in more serious circumstances. I also tried very hard to get myself accepted into boys' football teams, but without success.

But, in the same way that I was lucky to find a judo club with competitive aspirations, I found that the Hull Brewery team was also bent upon sporting success. In the following year, 1976, Hull Brewery won all the main national titles, and did much the same the following year. I was nicknamed 'The Whippet' at football, because I was still not yet a teenager, yet playing with women in their twenties. In the 1976–77 season I had trials for the England women's team and got through the first selection procedure, but was unable to attend the following selection because of a judo event. In any case, the England manager told me that I was still rather too small for a women's team; I should keep it up and wait a little – but by the time that happened, my whole view of sport had changed.

From the beginning of my secondary school career, I had been attracted increasingly to athletics – cross country in the winter and track work in the summer, as well as team games. I joined the Hull Spartans Athletics Club and worked at my running and long jumping, and I remember my coach saying to me that if only I would dedicate myself to only one sport, I could make something in the way of success. But I was just enjoying myself in three main sports – football, athletics and judo – and I couldn't possibly

Demonstrating tap the ball at Hull City football ground in 1975.

make a choice. As it happened, the all-round training I received was tailor-made for a top-level judo career.

AJA Wins

In 1976, I won my club championships, plus an award for the best ippon throw, and the trophy for the best judo player of the year, as well as the AJA Area Championships and a bronze medal at the national team event.

The following year saw more judo success. I won the area championships of another of the smaller judo associations, the British Judo Council – who, incidentally, are unusual in that they allow armlocks and strangles at all junior levels – and was awarded the trophy for the best ippon throw. I was now 14 and travelling extensively with the National Dock Labour Board club. I won numerous local and area AJA and BJC championships, both at my own weight – which was now under 35 kilos – and at the weight above. One of the problems of judo clubs is that you often end up fighting your friends. This year, again, I only won the club trophy by beating my best friend, Kerry Thornton, which is not always easy.

The year's efforts came to a peak in Blackburn when I won the AJA National Championships at under 35 kilos. Although life on the judo road tends to mean that one competition blurs into another, I remember that one distinctly. The girl I was to meet in the final kept saying to me 'I'm going to beat you in the final . . . I'm going to beat you.' She never stopped. I pointed her out to my dad and told him that she was upsetting me. I didn't understand why she was saying it. He explained that she was only trying to get me worried, and once I understood, I stopped being nervous. I threw her for ippon with *morote-seoi-nage*.

I must say that my parents have always supported me. They travelled with me to competition after competition, and my dad always took me training. Many times he would get in from work, sit down to have a cup of tea, and I would say, 'Come on, dad, it's judo tonight. ' He always took me – though sometimes with a little grunt – but he never let me down.

My running was still very important to me at this time. In 1977 I won the Hull schools 800 metres and 1,500 metres, and came second in the long jump. I represented the county in the All-England Cross Country, and came 259th out of 702. The following year I cut that down to 159 out of 702. But more and more often, now, there was no question which sport would win when judo clashed with football or running, although I was still only doing two nights a week.

It was becoming increasingly clear that my real love was for judo, but I was slightly uneasy. The National Dock Labour Board club was a marvellous club for juniors, but as I approached 15 I could see that my days as a junior were coming to an end. The tradition in the NDLB was that when you reached senior level, you tended to help out with the kids, which was not really what I wanted to do. If the road to the top in women's football seemed a little unclear – I realised quite early on that women's football would never receive the kind of widespread recognition as men's football – judo in the AJA wasn't much clearer. Yet, like many juniors within the smaller associations, I remained remarkably unaware of what was happening, and what was possible, in the wider judo world. The AJA and the BJC seemed self-sufficient, enclosed worlds, and the successes of people like Brian Jacks didn't really penetrate.

The British Judo Association

My outlook changed completely when I went on a judo course run by Ellen Cobb of the British Judo Association. She explained to me that if I really wanted to get on, I had to join the BJA. It was not something I did immediately, but it became the obvious next step.

I liked the NDLB because it was a brilliant junior club with a good club atmosphere. Some of my best judo memories stem from the old call stand by the Hull Docks, and the basis of my tachiwaza undoubtedly stemmed from there. The coaches were well balanced, too: Jim Tanser was the rough one with the insistence on discipline, and Tom Jickells was more soft and placid. So it was with regret that I left the docks, and moved to the Hull Prison Officers' Judo Club, run by one of the prison officers, Charlie Thompson, and a younger Dan grade, Neil Witty.

Although I found the atmosphere and judo quite different, I had grown up a lot in the past 12 months, which could be seen by my first BJA medals. I won the Humberside Junior Championships at both under 52 kilos and the open weight.

But my first big eye-opener was the BJA Southern Area tournament at Crystal Palace, which remains an extremely competitive event to this day. Many people feel that a medal in the Southern Area is almost equivalent to a national medal.

The Crystal Palace Sports Centre itself horrified me, and I wasn't helped by being told that I was not ready for this competition. Whoever told me that was right, but I felt that I had to start somewhere, so I might as well jump off in the deep end. Perhaps also, inside myself, I felt that having won so much at the AJA, it couldn't be that different in the BJA. I was wrong.

The judo felt totally different, first and foremost because it was much more physical. In the AJA you took hold and the contest gradually began, with relatively gentle gripping. Suddenly, at Crystal Palace, I was confronted by girls who fought hard for the grips they wanted, and fought for the whole time. My much-loved *morote-seoi-nage*, which had worked for so long against opponents who moved relatively smoothly around the mat with me, was killed before I had even managed to turn. And my groundwork was virtually non-existent, because newaza was rather frowned upon in the AJA. All I could do was to stay out of trouble, but I felt as though I was being squashed like a ball.

The other problem was that I was accustomed to ippon and waza-ari scores only, but here had to contend with yukos and kokas. What's more, in the AJA there were no real restrictions on mat area and in one fight I received a keikoku for throwing out of the area. I had no idea of the intricacies of the red-line rule.

But I discovered I could fight – it was my fighting spirit that won me three fights, if I remember correctly. By the time the day was over I came away without a medal, but looking as though I had fought a war – I was covered in bruises, grazes and mat burns. It taught me that I had a lot of work to do. I had to make that decision: was I prepared to put the work in, in order to climb the BJA ladder, or was I going to give up and concentrate on athletics. My father said that it was definitely a different ball game, and that I had to make the decision for myself.

I went back to Hull thoughtful but not dismayed. I knew that I wouldn't give up, and I immediately started to do something about my groundwork. But at 15, I didn't feel I was under any pressure to make anything like a momentous decision. As far as I was concerned, I was still enjoying football and athletics, and I could continue to do them. I see from my scrap-book of 1978, that in addition to the judo, the Hull Brewery football side won the five-a-side competition in Prestatyn, came second in the All-England tournament and won the women's cup; and apart from coming 159th in the All-England Cross Country, I was a member of my school side that won the Schools' Basketball Team League.

The circumstances of my first BJA grading were also worth noting. I went for my first BJA grade in October, some time after fighting in my first competitions. I had reached brown belt in the AJA – and that was no easy feat, for in addition to the contesting, I had to do kata as well. But I was told that I had to be downgraded to orange belt which, in retrospect, was unnecessary. I didn't mind too much, because I wasn't so interested in grades. To me, judo was a sport, and what was important was how good you were and how you won your contest, not the colour of the belt around your middle. But my mother and father felt rather differently – they saw it only as something that I had achieved which was taken away. In any case, as soon as I went into a BJA grading, I went up to blue belt, so it didn't make much difference in the end.

I was much more pleased that in November I went down to London again, where I picked up a bronze medal in the National Under-16 Championships in Crystal Palace. All the work I had done in the intervening months seemed to have paid off and I felt that I was at least on the bottom rungs of the BJA ladder.

2 Early Successes

The year 1979 was very much a crossroads for me. For a start, it was the year I left school. Throughout my school career, I seemed to lead two lives. Inside school, I worked reliably without demonstrating any academic brilliance. I was always quiet and generally well-behaved, getting on with the work I was set. It was only outside that I went wild, particularly during my primary years and the first years of my secondary school. My idea of fun was to do a sponsored half-marathon, then come back and play a game of football. I was never interested in things like make-up, clothes or boys. Boys were the people I played football with, that was all, and clothes meant tracksuits or T-shirt and shorts. When I shared a room with my sister, Anita, her half of the room would be covered with Donny Osmond and other pop singers, and my half would be decorated with footballers.

I was just beginning to change a little at the time I left school. I decided that, although I knew I wanted to be involved in sports in one way or another, I should get a qualification, so I signed up for a secretarial course at the college of further education. And, for the next two years, I followed the course assiduously. I am a bit of a perfectionist, and although I wasn't really interested, I learned typing and shorthand, and other secretarial skills, somehow fitting all the homework around my increasingly demanding training schedule. After two years, much to the surprise of some of my tutors who were concerned with my increasing absences due to judo, I passed my diploma. I remember arriving home with it, putting it on the kitchen table and saying to my mother: 'There it is, but I will never use it.'

By the time I turned 16, I seemed to settle into the 52 kilos category, despite my height. I won the Yorkshire Championships at under 52 kilos, and presumed that it would be my normal category. But after leaving school, I spent a few months on the dole – I tried for some jobs, but I couldn't get enough time off to allow me to train – and started a more concentrated training pattern. I began to realise that instead of just doing various sports and surviving on all-round fitness, it was time that I trained to be fit. I started running far more extensively, and I seemed to lose weight without really trying. There had been times when I would run to judo, even during my AJA days, which involved about four miles (my poor father would follow me in the car), and I began to run regularly to my new club. In 1979 the Hull Prison Officers' Judo Club moved into a new sports centre, and was renamed the South Holderness Judo Club. It was about six miles from my home on the Bransholme estate, but I would run along the grass verges with my father again following patiently.

National Team Championships

My weight dropped to 48 kilos, and I entered and won the Humberside Championships, winning both the junior title and the under-21s. Although I was a junior, I was attending the Yorkshire and Humberside training sessions, and the coach, Sally Peake, picked me to fight for the Midland Area in the National Team Championships in June. She said I was not really ready for it, but the team was missing one player. She moved the 48 kilo player to 52 kilos, and I stepped in as the lightest weight. She told me to do my best, but obviously saw me as the weakest link in the team, which had established internationals such as Maureen Bennett and Dawn Netherwood. It was Dawn who looked after me – she became the first player in the area I really got to know.

The competition itself was quite a breakthrough for me. I won all my fights in the preliminaries, and in the final the result depended on me – I had to win for the team to take the championships. I did, and everybody offered to buy me a drink, but I didn't drink at the time and, what's more, I didn't even want to try.

After the team's success, it was decided to travel to an international competition in Spain – so long as the team members were able to contribute. This was my first time on an aeroplane and my first time abroad, and I was really looking forward to seeing foreign competitors. I won my first two fights, and was then beaten. But I felt that, once again, I had made another important step in judo. Fighting in the Southern Area had shown me what the world of the BJA was like, and then fighting abroad in Spain had given me an insight into the wider international world of judo. Each was a significant hurdle; although I realised that I was a long way from being a successful international, this did not dampen my keenness. Before I could realistically think in terms of winning abroad, I had to deal with certain difficult individuals at home – not least my great rival in the Midlands area, Sandy Fry. On the weekend I arrived back from Spain, she beat me into silver place, totally confusing me with her constant attacks with *drop seoi-nage*.

Towards the end of the year, I found myself going more frequently to a different judo club, the Kingston Judo Club, in an old school nearer to my home. The reason was partly because I was getting quite a lot of help from Neil Witty, who changed clubs. The coach at Kingston Judo Club was Mike Joyce, who has advised and encouraged me from the day that I joined. He realised that I wanted to do something in judo, gave me access to the club so that I could train whenever I wanted, and introduced me to weight training – which was not something that many girls did at that time. But I knew that he was right and that I needed to get stronger.

Yet I was still managing to play football, and was a member of the Hull Brewery team that won the national five-a-side competition that year, managed by Lill and Bernard Matsell.

When I began my secretarial course at the college in the autumn, I was determined not to lose out on the fitness side. Apart from running to judo in the evening, I decided to get in some extra training early in the morning.

Throughout the winter I would get up at 6 a.m., no matter how wet or cold it was, wake my father, and go out for a run. I wanted my father with me because, frankly, I was afraid of the dark, and I think he was not too happy about me running around at that time without any supervision. But once again he never complained, but would stand on the end of the field shivering while I went round and round it on my runs. Such is parental support!

My First British Open

My fitness training obviously paid dividends, because I found myself worried by fewer and fewer players. In 1980 I won the Kingston Judo Club Championships and the Northern Area Open Championships, and then went down to London for my first British Open Championships. I got out of my pool fairly easily, but met the great Jane Bridge in the semi-finals.

Jane was European Champion at the time, and very much at the peak of her career – just months later she was to fly to New York to win the under 48 kilos category in the first World Judo Championships for women. She was also known as an outstanding stylist – which, to be truthful, was not a description that could be attached to Karen Briggs *circa* 1980. I had learned to fight and to scrap, and my reputation was very much as a terrier who would give anyone a battle. I was a brown belt at the time – I got my first kyu in the summer of 1979 – and Jane was, of course, a black belt, but that didn't worry me. Her technique, however, did.

I was simply outclassed. Though I started well, scrapping away as I normally did, she quickly learned to contain me, then threw and armlocked me. And that was that. I knew I was up against a player who was technically far in advance of me, but I was, nevertheless, very pleased with my performance on that day. I came back through the *repêchage*, winning a bronze medal and beating some good foreign opposition. It was obvious that I was beginning to make an impression. Jane went on to win the gold medal, beating Ann Lof of Sweden in the final. Interestingly, I stood on the bronze medal platform of the podium with my old rival Sandy Fry, who had come through on the other side of the *repêchage*. That victory podium gave me the clear message: the girls I had to beat in Britain were Sandy first, and then Jane. Each was a definite rung on the ladder to the top.

National Squad Training

By now, I was training quite intensely, but very often alone. I would do simple weights – working with dumb-bells and fairly light free weights – as well as skipping, sit-ups and press-ups. Mike Joyce, who was undoubtedly one of the best coaches in the area, would advise me, and I was quite happy to work on my own. I was still terribly shy and hardly spoke to anyone. The contrast between my uninhibited aggression on the mat and my diffident mouse act off it must have bewildered Roy Inman, the manager of the British women's team, when he invited me to my first national squad training shortly after my bronze in the British Open.

It was held at Pinewood, one of the leading junior judo clubs in the country, and it took me eight hours to get there. I remember being mortified with embarrassment, not least because I had a little blue suitcase – and all the other girls had sports bags. As soon as I got there I rang up my mother to tell her that I was the only one with a suitcase, and she sympathised, but pointed out that there wasn't very much she could do about it, except promise that she would get me a sports bag when I got back.

The training itself was just as bad. I didn't understand a thing that was going on. All the techniques seemed so incredibly complex, especially the groundwork rolls which were completely strange to me. I got my arms and legs in all the wrong places.

I didn't have a clue about crash-mat work – everyone else seemed so good technically, and I felt completely incompetent. Even the fitness was a problem, despite the extra work that I had done on my own. And whenever Roy Inman came to me and asked me how I was getting on, or if I understood, I would just look at the mat or the ceiling – he seemed so high to me. I didn't want anyone to talk to me, expect Dawn who I knew from my area. I only felt at home in the randori, when I could fight – though even there I got confused when Roy put me on with Jane and told me to try picking up her legs, simulating the style of one of her main opponents from abroad. I didn't know what I was doing.

When I got home afterwards, I slept for a full day, and I still felt terrible. And it was years, literally years, before I came to terms with Roy, and managed to look at him face to face. Now I try to remember what that was like when I encounter a new squad member on her first training weekend, when she is confused by drills that are second nature to me, and when I get bruised and battered by basic throwing practices – basic, that is, to those of us accustomed to Roy's ideas.

Establishing my Fighting Base

It was now some two years since I had joined the BJA, and my judo was certainly changing. The days of regular ippon scores from a clean *morote-seoi-nage* seemed to be over, and I was becoming more of a scrapper. I began to score more with *ouchi-gari* – a natural development against a strong defence to my *seoi-nage* attack. But I was prepared to win at any cost, picking up a leg here, pulling down there. I still produced ippon scores, but more because I would bewilder and confuse my opponent through constant attacking than by an incisive technique – that was to come later. I scored quite regularly with footsweeps, and then would win with a strangle on the ground, my groundwork had improved from its non-existent state with the help of Neil Witty at the Kingston Judo Club, who spent hours with me doing newaza turnovers. It was also at this time that my fighting posture –

slightly bent and always pressing forward – first established itself, largely, I think, because I was accustomed to fighting much bigger opponents at the Kingston Judo Club.

I knew I lacked the kind of clarity of technique displayed by Jane Bridge, but I didn't worry about it – it was almost as if I was conscious of the fact that at this stage in my career I had to secure a fighting base, and I would be able to shape it and hone it later on, which is essentially what happened. As I look back on this chapter in my judo development, I can only say that it was as crucial as the technical improvements that came later.

I won the Consett Open Northern Area gold medal, and came back down to Crystal Palace (I was beginning to know it well) in November to win the National Under-18s 48 kilos title. But it was Sandy Fry and Jane Bridge I was really interested in, so, curiously perhaps, I remember the National Team Championships of that year more clearly. They gave me a chance to face the great Jane Bridge, and on an occasion when the actual outcome of our contest would not affect the team result – we were losing anyway.

Sally Peake, the team coach, told me just to go out and do my best. I went out and scrapped as well as I had ever done. I remember thinking at the time that I was doing quite well, and in the event I managed to hold Jane to a draw. I was absolutely jubilant. As soon as I came off the mat, I got on the telephone to Mike Joyce and said: 'You'll never guess what . . . I just drew with Jane Bridge.' He replied: 'God, that's good,' and must have felt that he really did have the possibility of a British Champion in his club.

Now I view that fight very differently. I know what it must have felt like to Jane, who was interested in the technical aspects of judo, to have a young, rough and aggressive fighter come out and just try to pull her around. Never in a month of Sundays could I have thrown her in that way, while at the same time the sheer aggressive activity just blocked any decent move that Jane might make. I now find myself on the receiving end of young fighters like that, whose only concern is to topple you from the number one spot, regardless of how it is done. It is not pleasant, but it is one of the penalties of being successful. It is a syndrome that manifests itself in all sports, from combat sports to athletics, and probably, in its way, in something like snooker too.

I was young and hungry and not afraid of anyone – only the dark. Put me in a lighted club or stadium, and I would fight anyone at any time. That is what I felt like on that day, and it was then that I realised that neither Jane Bridge nor anyone else was unbeatable. I remember talking to Dawn Netherwood after the competition – we got a bronze, by the way – and she said she was going to America for the World Championships. It flashed through my mind that if I wanted to get to those places, I would have to train much harder.

In a way, that was the time I began firmly to reject football. It was obvious that there was a limited future in it, and in any case, judo was proving even more demanding than I had anticipated. That year, 1980, the Hull Brewery were again the league winners, and the seven-a-side winners, but my interest was waning. Athletics too was taking more of a back seat, though

I often wonder what would have happened had I decided to put my main efforts into my running. Even now I am not quite sure whether I turned to judo because I seemed to be attaining greater national success there than in running, or whether it was a natural enjoyment of judo as a combat sport – the immense and even primitive challenge of a fight.

I had an interesting diversion taking part in the Daily Mirror Champion Children of the Year Competition, run by Dr Barnardos. My brother Michael entered me and I came third – winning the chance of a trip to London to an awards reception with the Archbishop of Canterbury.

But once I heard that Jane had won the World Championships in New York in December, and felt confident that I had the ability to beat her, I knew in my heart what I was going to concentrate on.

3 First International Championships

The year 1981 began on a good note. I won the Senior Trials in Crystal Palace, winning most of my fights with ippon, and beating Sandy Fry into the bargain. What's more, I accumulated sufficient points to be awarded the coveted black belt on 31 January. In fact, because I regarded judo so much as a sport, similar to athletics or gymnastics, it didn't really mean much to me. I know that for many people getting a black belt is one of the high points of a judo career. But there was no sense of a blatant, established heirarchy like that in all the other sports I was involved in, so I couldn't really see its importance. As far as I was concerned, any belt would do. On the other hand, the black belt has a very strong tradition in judo, and I can see nothing wrong with maintaining it. From time to time I have been upgraded, although most of my contest points come from major competitions rather than grading contests.

Setting my Goals

My eyes were firmly fixed on the top sport of the under 48 kilos category, even though Jane Bridge seemed to be well settled there having won the World Championships in December 1980 in New York. I suppose that that kind of total belief in yourself is a necessary quality of a world champion or a leader in any human activity. And perhaps, in women's judo, it was not so unjustified, because straight after winning her title, Jane Bridge stopped for quite a while. It was as if she had pushed herself to the peak, and, having no higher peaks to climb, went in to decline. She said she was just having a rest and would be back, and certainly that is exactly what she tried to do, although, as we all know, it is much harder to stage a come-back than it is to reach your goal in the first place. Meanwhile, I went into every worthwhile competition I could find. It meant an extremely active life, of course, trying not just to maintain my fitness, but to improve it, as well as to develop my judo – and trying to keep up my work with my secretarial studies. I remember that I often had to miss audio typing lessons late on Fridays because I would be travelling for competitions, but somehow I managed to get some practice in, and I even passed that in the end.

European Championships and Beyond

I won the Edinburgh Open and the North of England competition, but by now I was really looking to my career abroad. I had yet to be involved in a full international, and to go straight in to the European Championships in Madrid in March should have been a nerve-racking experience. But it is much easier going in as a relative novice with nothing much expected of you, than going in as the favourite. I am now convinced that you become more nervous for the big events after some successful years, not less nervous.

I didn't have an auspicious preparation. As has happened so often for the Europeans, I was injured before, this time suffering from a wrist injury sustained in practice, which meant that I was off the mat for about three weeks just prior to the event.

It didn't seem to affect my performance, however, though it just might have made the difference between winning a finalist's medal or a bronze. I won my pool fairly easily, and progressed through the knockout, beating Ann Lof of Sweden, who used to give Jane Bridge a lot of trouble, on the way. My hardest fight came in the semi-final, against the eventual silver medallist, Ann de Novellis of Italy. We were quite evenly matched, but her fitness was suspect and she wilted in the second half of the fight. Yet at full time she went through to the final on a split decision, while I had to fight for a bronze medal, which I won.

I was pleased with the bronze, but annoyed with myself that I did not make the final. Only a few times in my career have I lost in the final, and I believe now that, had I beaten De Novellis, I would have won the European title on my first attempt. Nevertheless, it was a sucessful event for the British team as a whole, with Ann Hughes winning the light middleweight title and Loretta Doyle winning a silver in the featherweight. I smile when I look back on that event, for I was still extremely naïve. I shared a hotel room with Loretta, and I remember persuading her to warm up in the bedroom so that the opponents should not see our techniques.

I noted that in *Judo* magazine, Colin McIver, later to become manager of the British men's team, wrote that my wins in the early rounds were 'very impressive' and he continued: 'I have no doubt that she will improve over the next year and become a very successful competitor.'

Just to show how competition-mad I was at the time, just ten days after winning the European bronze, I was fighting in a competition again, although perhaps that was slightly therapeutic – to rid myself of the frustration of not making the final. I won.

I did not have it all my own way in Britain in 1981. Sandy Fry beat me on a decision in a tense final of the Yorkshire and Humberside Senior Championships, but a couple of months later I gained my revenge. At the British Closed Championships at Crystal Palace in July I met her again and this time had the measure of her, throwing her for two yukos and two kokas. Never again was she to cause me difficulty.

Shortly afterwards I was selected to go to the Paris Tournament, but I had injured my back. In fact I had trained with a bad back for quite some years and had worn a back support every time I went on the mat for at least four years. The prospect of going to Paris, and the anxiety that if I told the team manager I was injured, it would affect possible selection in the future, made me decide to keep quiet about my back injury. I went, fought badly, and didn't get out of my pool.

Roy asked me why and I told him. When he discovered that I was injured before Paris, he said: 'You stupid girl, why didn't you tell me?' and packed me straight off to the medical division.

I still felt terribly shy and inhibited in front of Roy. I would never talk directly to him, never look at him face to face – always up at the ceiling or down at the floor. I felt mortified with fear and embarrassment every time he approached me. And he misunderstood, I think. I remember him saying once – though this was perhaps after I won my first world title: 'It doesn't matter if you don't like me, so long as you do the work.' It wasn't as if I actively disliked him; I found him rather overpowering off the mat, although on the mat I began to feel easier with him. I now acknowledge that I learned an enormous amount from him, and that we have a rather odd, even special love-hate relationship that has proved a strangely creative one.

And I must say that my decision to hide the injury at Paris did not stop him selecting me for other internationals. I went to the Dutch Open Championships in September, and won the gold medal. I was particularly pleased because it was a giant trophy.

Although by this time I had virtually stopped doing other sports seriously, I still enjoyed things like running. But in September, more for personal interest than anything else, and without any special training whatsoever, I entered the Humber Bridge Marathon. I surprised myself by coming in at 3 hours 47 minutes 58 seconds – winning an award as the second lady from a non-athletic club, and an award as the youngest lady finisher. I was 18.

I enjoyed the diversion of the BBC television series *It's a Knockout*. I did the fitness test trials for the local team, saying I was 18, although the trials were in February and my birthday was not until April. When I passed, I admitted my true age to Tony Taylor who was looking after the team (it was Tony who later employed me at Hull's new sports centre) but he pointed out that I would be 18 on the day of the first event, so my place was secured. We won the first local event, and then went to Yugoslavia for an international event in June, where we were rather disappointed to come fifth. It was a busy time because I was taking my final secretarial exams – I had to take one paper in the lecturer's house immediately after getting back from Yugoslavia. I passed my secretarial diploma well before I really knew whether I would make it to the top in judo – but I simply wasn't cut out for a desk job.

I fought for the Yorkshire and Humberside team that won the National Team Championships that year, and I must pay tribute to the help given to me by Sally Peake, the area team manager, during this time.

The shadow of Jane Bridge, however, still existed in the 48 kilo division. I had expected to meet her in the British Open in October, but she failed to make the weight, and fought in the under 52 kilos category. It was still a good day for me, with a series of ippons from throws and strangles, including throwing Ann de Novellis for yuko and then a koka, to show that I really could beat her, despite the European result. I then strangled Ann Bechepay of France with *okuri-eri-jime* and once again threw Sandy Fry four times to win the final. I felt in very good form indeed.

The Canada Cup

This was further confirmed at the last tournament of the year, the Canada Cup in Quebec in December, where I met, for the first time, my great French rival Marie-France Colignon. We came to grips in the final, and during a groundwork flurry, I strangled her with *okuri-eri-jime*. Diane Bell also won, and after the competition she and I – easily the most innocent girls on the squad in worldly matters – got quite drunk for the very first time.

I will remember Canada for other reasons too. It was an extremely exciting time for me, because I had never been out of Europe. I told my mother that I had been selected to go to Canada and that, as it was winter and would be snowing heavily, the BJA letter said that I would need warm clothing and boots. I had finished college and was on the dole, which really meant being supported by my parents, and my mother said that she didn't have enough money to buy boots and equipment. It didn't worry me too much because I was going there to do judo, and I knew I would manage, but as it turned out my mother got some money together. We went out shopping for a coat and boots, which were not cheap. In the end we bought a duffle coat, known at the time as my Paddington coat because of the children's story about Paddington Bear. I thought it was fine.

But after the competition, when we went skiing for the first time, I discovered that everybody but me had ski jackets. I wore my Paddington coat and Roy said I looked like a witch coming down the slopes, which upset me a little as my mother had saved up to buy me the coat or I wouldn't have had one at all. Now when I think about it I laugh, but at the time I was quite sensitive.

After the euphoria of winning the event, of skiing and getting drunk for the first time, and generally being treated like top athletes, as is commonplace on the other side of the Atlantic, I returned to earth, and Britain, with a bang. I was informed when I arrived that I had lost my supplementary benefit for being out of the country. My whole family regarded that decision rather bitterly – after representing my country, this was the reward.

4 World Champion

Training in Hull

Although women's judo was now firmly established on the international sporting calendar, it was still regarded as the poor relation, and men's judo not only took the lion's share of public attention, but commanded a much larger slice of the sport's grants. This was true throughout the judo world, but for all Britain's standing as one of the leading nations in women's judo, there was very little financial support. There was no way I could apply for a grant to allow the full-time training schedule that I needed to follow if I was to have a fighting chance of getting to the top, and staying there, at an international level. Like many British athletes, but particularly in judo, where Britain has traditionally done well abroad despite basic facilities at home, I had to go through the rather inappropriate routine of claiming unemployment benefit, while actually working extremely hard.

I was living at home, of course, and my parents were as supportive as always. And I began to get small, encouraging signs of support. I had a small grant from the Yorkshire and Humberside Area, and I lived frugally. I didn't really have a great interest in boyfriends and most of my friends came from the judo world now. In any case, I still felt more comfortable in tracksuits and jeans than in skirts. I even disliked the uniform – complete with skirt – that we had to wear when travelling as a team.

And I still felt very much a girl from Hull, being relatively ill at ease in any circumstances other than when jogging through the streets of a strange town 'getting a sweat' just prior to a weigh-in, or fighting on the mat itself. In fact, I was doing so much running and training at this time that my weight had dropped quite dramatically. Whereas just a couple of years before I was still comfortably in the 52 kilo category, I now found myself tipping the scales at 46 kilos or sometimes even 45. I had to begin to watch that I didn't dip even lower. By the time I was 18 my figure was settling into its adult form. Curiously, I seemed to have lost most of my weight from my bust, which was considerably smaller at 18 and 19 than at 16 and 17. Otherwise, the intensive training didn't seem to affect me, although, like most judo players, I always seemed to be carrying around with me a varying collection of minor injuries – bruised toes, bent fingers, torn finger nails, necks rubbed raw from the judogi collars, and wrenched muscles.

I would follow the routine of early morning runs, then fitness work down in the Kingston Judo Club, doing weights, circuit training – and suppling. At that first squad training, I had been horrified to find out how stiff I was in comparison with someone like Jane Bridge, and I knew I had to correct it. I even went to a few karate classes to get some hints on suppling routines, and then I established a regular pattern of nearly an hour a day doing stretching exercises. I didn't miss a day and worked hard, though it is easy to skimp on stretching, and within three months I saw some dramatic improvements. I will never be as supple as many women on the judo mat, like Jane or Dawn Netherwood, but I am supple enough. In fact, one of my techniques, my *te-guruma* counter, depends on my suppleness.

Challenging Jane

I enjoyed myself at home as usual during Christmas 1981, but even at the height of the festivities, my mind would flicker constantly to the coming year. I knew that this was going to be perhaps my most crucial year, for it culminated in October with the World Championships in Paris, and I desperately wanted to be there. But first I had to earn my place, and to do that I had to beat Jane Bridge.

Jane was not only the reigning World Champion – she was also respected throughout the judo world for her technical accomplishment. In comparison, I was still the scrapper-upstart, despite my European bronze medal from Madrid. I was less in awe of her now, for I had practised with her many times at squad training and knew that I could defend against her, even throw her. But she was still the World Champion. At all the internationals, when people saw my name on the pool sheets they would ask: 'Is that really Briggs, or Jane Bridge?' I couldn't get away from her shadow.

We met, as we had to, at the British Trials in Crystal Palace in January. For a year I had won virtually everything in Britain – and the trend continued, for I beat her, two kokas to one, although I had to come from behind to do it. After two minutes I was ahead on attacks, until Jane caught me with an *ouchi-gari* for a koka. I answered with a similar technique to level the score, and then edged ahead on another knock-down. The number one spot on the British squad was mine.

But, understandably, the team manager felt that it was not a sufficiently dominating win to secure my place as the leading British bantamweight international. Roy sent us both to Goslar, the West German Open, to see who would come out on top this time. I remember that Jane and I watched each other throughout the day, racing to see who could finish off opponents on each side of the draw more quickly. There were some devastating wins from both of us that day, and few fights in those early rounds lasted more than a minute.

And then we met in the final. This time I won more decisively. I footswept Jane in the opening 20 seconds and was awarded a yuko. A year before I would have continued fighting furiously, but I had learned something about tactics and mat sense. I played the rest of the fight far more cagily, defending most of the time, not giving Jane an inch with which to develop some of her smooth, beautiful techniques. It was a mature performance, and the West German title, but more importantly, my position as the leading British 48 kilo player was confirmed.

Jane Bridge, 1980 World Champion (under 48 kilos) – first of all a rival and now a good friend.

European Championships in Oslo

A month later I was back on the plane with the full British team, this time heading for the European Championships in Oslo. I felt much more experienced, yet more nervous than usual – not least because Roy had told me: 'Now that I have picked you and not Jane, you had better win.' I knew I had improved technically – I was beginning to be more aware of the technical implications of contests, rather than relying on fitness and aggression. But I also felt that the improvements had come so quickly that I wasn't sure whether they were totally secure.

On this occasion I need not have worried. I strangled my first East German opponent, and relied on my fitness and aggression to win a decision over Marie-France Colignon, whom I had beaten rather more easily in Canada a few months before. I was delighted to find, then, that my opponent in the final was none other than Ann De Novellis – again. After gaining two early kokas with a footsweep and an *ouchi-gari*, I threw her on her side for yuko, and that was enough. I was jubilant. Still only 18, I was European Champion and felt confident that, barring injury and the kind of mistake that everyone can and does make from time to time, the world title was a real possibility.

I also began to realise that I could produce my best at the most difficult times. Most sports champions know of rivals who, in training or in the small events, can sparkle with technique or that extra speed, but who cannot stand the stress of the top event. I was fortunate, it seemed, in being able to get better the more testing the conditions became, not worse. It was a factor that has played a crucial role in my success over the years. It was noticeable first, perhaps, in those team competitions for Yorkshire and Humberside when, with the result relying on me, a newcomer, I produced the necessary win. And now it showed that, even at European level, it still applied. But would it also apply at world level? That was the one thing I didn't know.

I returned – with Loretta having won another silver medal, beaten for the second year running by the Austrian Edith Hrovat – and within two weeks was competing again, in Edinburgh. The competitions came thick and fast, with wins in Scotland and in the Northern Open. That year came other wins – the Humberside Championships, the Midland Area, the National Team Championships (representing Yorkshire and Humberside, of course), as well as the Austrian Open and the Dutch Open. It seemed like non-stop competition, but this is the kind of frenetic life that teenagers on the way up to the top seem to thrive on.

Finding a Job

But it was not as simple as it sounds on paper. For a start, my circumstances had changed. I disliked living on the dole, more on principle than because I felt I was not earning a living. I knew that I was working as hard as most people in full-time jobs, if not harder, so to be registered as unemployed was something of a lie. The trouble was that whenever I applied for jobs and explained the amount of time I needed to take off for training and competitions, I was really a non-starter in formal employment terms. In addition to that, I really didn't want to work in a formal nine to five job, although I was suitably qualified. I tried it once, but left after a few days.

The opening of the newly-built Woodford Sports Centre in Hull, however, seemed to offer a better opportunity. It was within the sports area that I wanted, and offered shift work, with some flexibility concerning my training and competitions. I started work there in April 1982 as a sports hall assistant, doing everything from supervising and taking a few fitness classes, to laying out equipment. I quite enjoyed the work and the experience of being 'at work', with people to talk to – training full time can be a surprisingly solitary existence. I found the shift hours rather difficult – including the many late shifts of 3 p.m.–11 p.m., not least because they interfered seriously with my judo training. The receptionist at the sports centre, Cath Atwood, was seriously worried that I was overdoing things. But for the following 18 months or so I was working less hours at the Woodford Sports Centre, fitting in my training where I could. As I write I am still attached formally to the centre – and I go in frequently to do my weight training – but I am very grateful for the freedom given to me by the Hull leisure services, who have kept me on the staff on a part-time basis, despite my training commitments.

Discovering Tomoe-nage

Though I was even more closely tied to Hull now, I still managed to get down South for squad training – something which became increasingly important as the World Championships drew nearer. It was on one of these weekends early in the year that, for the first time, I was to come across the technique which transformed my judo – *tomoe-nage*.

From time to time Roy livened up the squad training by inviting guest instructors, and on this particular occasion he brought along Kerrith Brown. At that time, he was the top British 65 kilo player who had yet to make his mark abroad, although he was to win a European junior title, and a European silver medal at senior level.

By this time my judo had improved. I had much more to offer than simply aggression, fitness and what one journalist described as 'a piercing determination to win'. My *morote-seoi-nage* from the old AJA days seemed to have changed into a *tai-otoshi*, or even a *seoi-otoshi* when the occasion demanded, although it was only later that I really began to develop it quite clinically. I must acknowledge a little help from Brian Jacks here – I picked up some useful pointers about *tai-otoshi* from a course I attended where he taught. I also had a useful *ouchi-gari*, and no end of pick-ups, though I mainly used those as counters, with the exception of a *kouchi-gari* leg grab – dignified by Roy by the Japanese usage of *ashi-dori*. My groundwork had also developed so that I felt relatively safe on the ground. At the beginning of my international career, Roy used to tell me to finish my opponents off on the ground once I had thrown them, but I lacked the confidence. I would simply stand up feeling that I didn't have any idea what I was doing. By the beginning of 1982, I still wasn't what I would call a groundwork technician, but I was learning quickly to see opportunities and to be able to make the most of them. However my favourite technique was still to jump on a back and slide my hands in for *okuri-eri-jime*.

Then Kerrith demonstrated *yoko-tomoe-nage, side tomoe-nage*. *Tomoe-nage* is perhaps the most famous of all judo techniques, and I had known it for as long as I can remember. After all, it features in more thrillers and westerns than any other single judo throw. In my AJA club, I remember one boy who used to do it quite well, in the classic way – taking his opponent straight over the top.

It was just because it was so well known that it was rarely seen in top competition. But Kerrith showed a different version, a *side tomoe-nage* – so called because instead of attacking underneath your opponent in a straight line, you spun slightly to the side. The subtle change of direction made a dramatic difference, nullifying the standard defences.

At first glance, what Kerrith showed seemed rather complicated. I was still green enough to view with some suspicion modern, complex techniques. But Roy told us try it with our partners.

As soon as I tried it, I knew it was for me. Something just clicked. I seemed to feel absolutely at home, spinning in sideways at speed and taking my opponent over the top or slightly to the side. In a way it was rather curious because I had never specialised in dropping throws or sacrifice throws of any kind. Whereas the *drop seoi-nage* was the most popular throw in women's judo at the time – and probably still is – I would never do it. It may have been something to do with my formal training at the AJA, where a *drop seoi-nage* was regarded as sloppy judo, but I have never been comfortable doing it. I was even more bemused because I was the only member of the squad to take to *side tomoe-nage* – none of the others liked it at all, and even now I am the only one to use it regularly.

Yoko-tomoe-nage, however, was a sacrifice throw that seemed to make the most of my natural movement patterns. I found that not only was I able to spin into position with a fast, fluent movement, but that I visualised the attacking pattern as a complete circle, so that if it failed, I found myself back on my feet again. Despite my reliance on it for over five years of top competition – and on one or two occasions I have tried it in rather desperate circumstances – I have never been penalised for illegal dropping or dragging down.

That squad training felt like a breath of fresh air to me. It was obvious, and not only to me, that I had stumbled on a gold seam. One of the coaches called Roy over to my corner where I was practising it and said: 'Come and have a look at this.'

Of course, throws don't come easily in contest, however smooth they may feel in practice. I went back to Hull excited, and tried it on all the juniors. It worked virtually from the start. It took more time to develop *yoko-tomoe* into a throw that would work against useful seniors, but there was no question about its potential for me.

I had, for some time, kept a detailed notebook about all the things I learned at squad training, and then elsewhere, and *yoko-tomoe* began to figure more and more prominently in it. But it was not ready to use in the European Championships in Oslo, although it began to appear in domestic events.

World Championships Preparation

It was also not quite ready for my final tournament abroad before the World Championships, the French Open Championships in Paris in September. It was, to me, just one more small stepping-stone – but it was only with hindsight that I realised how important it actually was. The big victories in the sports world are built on the small defeats.

Everything seemed to be going as normal. I won my first five fights with ippon, and was a yuko up on Marie-France Colignon in the final, as well as a handful of kokas. I was extremely confident, and I decided to try something quite flashy. I attacked her with a right *osoto-gari* while she was controlling my head, and she simply turned to throw me for ippon with *osoto-gari* in return. It was a very long time since I had been thrown like that – or it seemed a long time – and although I was depressed immediately afterwards, I knew it had happened not because Colignon was an outstanding opponent, but because I had made a mistake.

I also knew that I had learned more from that defeat for the coming World Championship than if I had won again. I had personally experienced a golden rule – never attack with a rear throw against an arm over the top. I have very rarely made the same mistake twice, so while it was a small blow to my pride, it was worth the pain. After all, it could have been the final of the World Championships.

Ironically, it was an extraordinary championships for the British team as a whole. We got five girls into the final, and everyone got a silver.

Two weeks later, I was in another final – and this time I made no mistake. It was the British Open, and I faced a friend of mine, Sharon Rendle, who was competing for Grimsby Judo Club, although she comes from Hull, and who had oscillated between the under 48 kilo and the under 52 kilo category. She had done well to get to the final in a 30-nation tournament since she was only 16, but I knew her judo very well – she had fought at under 52 kilos in the Yorkshire and Humberside team that won the national team championships that year. She submitted to one of my strangles.

I was already feeling in peak form, partly because I had taken a break from my job and moved down to London in order to train daily under the tutelage of Roy Inman. He wanted to gather a group of us who could run together, do weights together, do all the judo training together, and then do the randori practice in the evenings at Fairholme Judo Club, his club in New Road, Bedfont. He had very clear ideas on how women should train. In many ways it was his pioneering ideas that brought such consistent success to the British women's squad.

I understand that when he first became involved with the women's squad, in 1977, he taught judo as he knew it – which was men's judo, relying on a lot of explosive power throws. But by the time I came on the scene, he had completely reassessed his approach, and was now working far more on speed, timing and rotation than power work. Although there were many indications that he was on the right track – not least Jane's world title in 1980 – the consistency of top results achieved by women under his eye from 1980 to the present day says it all. It certainly wasn't a simple case of Roy being graced with a group of judo players of exceptional natural gifts. Most of us were made, not born into the world champions we became, although perhaps that is more true of some than others.

Roy also had to work with an establishment that was not too keen on pouring money into the women's squad. This is an understatement. He was constantly wheeling and dealing to raise money for trips, for grants, for training equipment, for training sessions. He got better at it as time went on – helped, it must be said, by the medals that we all won – but at the start of the run-up to the 1982 World Championships he could only offer us the facilities of the Fairholme Club. Ann Hughes already lived in a flat nearby, as did Dawn Netherwood, who had won a world silver medal in 1980 in the middleweight (under 66 kilo) category.

But Diane Bell and I agreed to come down and sleep in the reception area of the dojo, and we were joined, for a time, by Loretta Doyle, until she could take it no longer. It was not easy waiting for everyone to leave the dojo in the evening so that we could drag out our camp beds and get some sleep. Nor was it easy to wake up with the sight of the dojo in our eyes, day after day, week after week. It does not appear such a hardship, particularly as were still in our teens and aiming to make our permanent mark on the international record books. The impersonality of it began to get through to us in the end, however – it was like sleeping on the floor of a public building.

But it did concentrate our minds. We worked extremely hard – like myself, Diane does not shirk from the graft, though it took me a little while to convince her and Ann that running was enjoyable. And, for those of us who did not have too much of a problem with our weight, we had the best meat the local butcher could provide – courtesy of Roy Inman. He knew that we didn't have enough money to eat very well, and he felt strongly that we couldn't do a lot of heavy physical work without good nourishment. I think he was also a little worried about the way my weight was dropping down to 45 kilos so regularly. So he told us we could order anything we liked from the butchers, and he would pick up the bill at the end of the week. He contributed in other ways too. He found accommodation for Diane and myself with parents of members of Fairholme's junior section, and he even got hold of an old car for us, which would allow us to be a little more independent. In fact, despite the generosity of the family with whom we lived, it wasn't ideal because both Diane and I felt a little uneasy, spreading around the home our sopping training clothes and generally making too strong an impression on the home life. So we moved back to the club house, and just knuckled down to the training.

Not surprisingly I was working a lot on my *tomoe-nage* now, devising as many ways as possible to develop it, even though it is a difficult throw to do a lot of uchikomi on. In the end, I decided that most of the work had to be done in the randori sessions, and this is where Roy's insistence that we practised with the juniors before the evening session really paid off.

Junior boys of around 15, Roy felt, were a particularly good practice because they were strong and fit enough to stand the pace, and, if they were blue or brown belts, skilled enough to offer a challenge; yet they were not worried by being thrown. Unlike many men, they did not feel that they had lost face if they were caught in a good throw, so they did not walk around the mat strong-arming you in a rather negative defence. I attempted *tomoe-nage* again and again to try to establish that smooth, circular action that is the essence of the throw, and by 5 December, the day of the World Championship in Paris, it was ready.

The Competition

In my first fight, I threw Verguillas of Spain with *yoko-tomoe-nage* after about a minute. My second fight, against Nakahara of Japan was all over in 28 seconds – this time with *tomoe-nage* for ippon. I also beat Majdan of Poland well before time, although it was through the combination of a yuko from a throw, finishing off with ippon through *yoko-shiho-gatame.*

I seemed to find myself in the final of the World Championships quite suddenly. My opponent was Marie-France Colignon again, but I wasn't too worried by the result of our last meeting, even though she had won all her preliminary fights with ippon on that day as well. I was fairly confident that I had lost because of my fault, not a move initiated by her. But she had improved herself – it was quite clear she had been studying videos of me, and had learned to contain me.

I attacked from the start, and for the first time I couldn't really make a strong impression on her. This was not so surprising. She was in the Stade de Coubertin, in Paris, arguably the most exciting judo venue in which to perform, because although the French crowd are understandably partisan, they do appreciate good judo, from wherever it comes.

Our styles are so different. She stands very upright – which is not good for my *tomoe-nage* – while I crouch, leading on the right foot. She attacks mainly with throws such as *uchi-mata,* while I try a range of techniques. After one and a half minutes of the five-minute final, there was no score. Then, in a swift attack, I managed to score a koka with a *yoko-tomoe-nage.* Remembering the Paris tournament a few months earlier, I was careful not to become reckless. I attacked again, but was mainly concerned to smother all her attempts to level the score, and when the bell for full-time went, my koka was the only score on the board.

I had done it. My main ambitions had been achieved – I held all the major judo titles for women in the world. I was particularly delighted because I had done it in front of my parents, who had travelled to Paris to watch, and my coach, Mike Joyce, from the Kingston Judo Club. They came to the hotel where the team was staying – with a bottle of champagne for me, though by that time I was pretty far gone anyway.

The celebrations went on through the night. It had been a good championships for Britain in other weight categories, for Loretta Doyle had also won a gold medal and her parents were also there to see her win. She

Loretta Doyle after winning the 1982 World Championships final against Yamaguchi of Japan.

The Paris World Championships, 1982 – I am throwing Madjan of Poland with *tomoe-nage* for ippon, which takes me into the finals.

had beaten her old rival Edith Hrovath in the first round on a split decision, and won another tactical victory in the final, against the very talented Kaori Yamaguchi of Japan. What's more, my training partner, Diane Bell, had won a bronze medal too, having beaten the Austrian Gerda Winklbauer.

Roy was delighted – he had been through a difficult first day which produced no medals at all, so he was as much relieved as anything else to see that all his ideas and his preparation had paid off.

The celebrations continued when I got home. The Kingston Judo Club had a big banner spread across the dojo, made, I was informed later, by my old training partner Neil Witty *before* I left for Paris – a bit too much like chancing fate. In addition, the Yorkshire and Humberside Area presented me with a silver rose bowl.

It was only as Christmas came that it sunk in that, at 19, I had won the World Championships. I had a wild time.

5 Staying on Top

Consolidating my Fitness

One of the by-products of my competition success was the accumulation of contest points for my 2nd Dan. I had gained sufficient points to move up a grade a few months after being awarded my 1st Dan in 1981, but it took more time to get around to doing the theory. I passed it in 1982, but again it wasn't something that I felt was particularly important. In 1983 I reached 3rd Dan (in September, although, again, I had the necessary contest points well before). I was more heartened to see the results of a fitness test I completed at a national squad training in the first weeks of 1983. This demonstrated clearly to me that perseverance in attaining what I felt was a good fitness level, largely on my own in Hull, was worth while. I came out top of the squad in most areas. Conducted by Peter Brown, the comment was: 'An excellent score which could represent the peak of physical fitness with some improvements.'

I was 19, and my weight was recorded at 46 kilos (although I was not dieting for a competition); my pulse rate was 52 at rest. Three of the five exercises came into the top bracket: 56 sit-ups in one minute; 83 push-ups (maximum number without rest), which exceeded the number suggested as the top mark expected; and 43 burpees in a minute, which also exceeded the total expected. I ran one and a half miles in 9 minutes 2 seconds, which put me in the second fitness level and my sprinting only made the third level, with 50 seconds for 5×60 metres. I was told I could improve by working more on sprints, with hill work, interval training and shuttles.

Incidentally, the men's squad did more or less the same test and I was interested to note that I came out slightly ahead of even Neil Adams.

I was convinced that one of the reasons for my fitness was the establishment of a fitness room in my house. One of the advantages of being the youngest but one child in a large family is that by the time I grew up, there was more room in the house. By this time my older brothers and my sister Anita had left home, and I was able to turn one of the bedrooms into a fitness centre.

I had an exercise bike in one corner, and a sit-up board in another; my father fixed a roll bar for strengthening wrists and fingers on the wall. I invested in a variety of weights and a judo mat, doing all my weight-lifting on the mat in the centre of the room. I would get up in the morning, go for a run, and often a swim as well, doing 50 lengths non-stop, and then go into the weights room. Of course I could still use the facilities of the Kingston Judo Club, which by now had moved into its own building. This move was partly helped, I think, by my success and that of others from the club, including Stuart Travis, Melody Haywood, Janice Witty and others.

But it was simpler for me to train at basic fitness in my own home. I even had a heater installed so that I could work up a good sweat during the winter when the room could get surprisingly cold. All around the wall I had various charts – the circuits I would do for that week, my detailed weight programme, and my bike programme. I even had an uchikomi programme, having fixed up straps and a belt on which I could turn on the wall, although as I write I must confess that it has been torn off for the umpteenth time. These houses were not made for this kind of punishment.

I was looking forward to enjoying 1983. The year after a World Championships is always more relaxed (or almost always – 1987 was to be an exception) because for women there is no big world event, although for the men, once every four years, there is the Olympic Games. So, perhaps I would be able to bask a little, and take things more easily after the intensity of years of struggling to make the top. Unfortunately, I didn't account for my personality.

I realised quite quickly that I am happiest when I am working hard, with my eyes fixed on a goal. Recently I have learned to take things more easily, and enjoy the quiet, non-competitive periods, but at 19 every competition was a major challenge for me. Just because I held the World and European titles, I didn't feel I could rest. Quite the opposite. I now had a position to maintain, and I felt I had to redouble my efforts. I knew I still lacked the kind of technical expertise I felt should go with my titles. By now I was much more than just a fit, aggressive fighter, but I needed to bring more and more clarity to my judo. I couldn't forget that, only three months or so before, I had been thrown for ippon because I made a technical error. I had learned from it, but I had to ensure that something like that would not happen again.

In any case, there was still the full programme of domestic competitions, although now I began to be a little more selective, missing out on some of the regional events in order to give myself time to work to a programme in preparation for the big ones. The year started, as usual, with the British Trials, which I won for the third time running.

European Championships in Genoa

The British Trials were followed, in March, by the 1983 European Championships, held in Genoa, Italy. This was the first time that I seriously encountered the nerves that face all world champions as they go back into competition after initial success. Suddenly, all eyes are on you, and so much is expected of you. In the event, totally unexpected circumstances produced such a private tragi-comedy that all minor interferences like nerves before the final became rather insignificant.

The route to the final was fairly easy. I threw and armlocked Greta Friedrickson of West Germany, threw and held down the Swedish girl in the second round, and then met for the first time a French girl who was to share the competitions with Colignon over the ensuing years – Fabienne

Boffin. I have had occasional difficulties with both, but this first meeting with Boffin should have been easy – I threw and armlocked her. But the referee had called a stop just as she submitted to the armlock – it took me a little while to maneouvre her into it – and, after some discussion, decided to allow the fight to continue. In the event I won anyway, with a yuko from a throw. This put me into the final against Anna Maria Valvano of Italy.

There was the usual break before the final, and I talked with the team members and watched Loretta fight her way to the final too, against Pascal Doger of France. About half an hour before we were due to go on, we decided to warm up, and, by accident, when Loretta was trying something out on Roy's suggestion, she half-threw me and severely banged my front teeth. Blood spurted out of my mouth, and one of the big teeth had loosened badly in the gum. I was fuming because it was so unnecessary, and the bleeding wouldn't stop. Roy told me to go and see Loretta who had gone out of the room because she was so upset that she was crying. I remember saying rather tartly: 'She's upset? What about me, look at the state of my mouth.' We were standing there, both crying, with me covered in blood and our names about to be called for the 1983 European Judo Championships finals. Roy was trying to calm us down, and it was at this point that Arthur Mapp, who won a bronze medal in the Olympics in 1980, but was then assistant to Roy, appeared. He turned round to me, pulled out his false tooth, and with a great gap in his mouth said: 'Don't worry, you can always get one of these.' That set me off even worse.

I remember going on to the mat with tears in my eyes from the pain in my mouth and my anger and frustration, and it clearly came through in my judo. I turned the Italian girl over almost immediately and held her down. No one would have been able to escape from my hold when I felt like that.

The affair ended well, because Loretta won too so in the evening we were both happy, World Champions and European Champions, and we could give each other a cuddle and start laughing.

Work with the Squad

During the build-up to the 1982 World Championships I knew Diane better than any other member of the squad, partly because we were both 'new girls.' But as 1983 unfolded, I began to get on well with Ann Hughes who was, perhaps, a better training partner for me. Although she was three weight categories higher at the time, she was smaller than Diane who was really a bit too tall.

I started to train with Ann more, not least because I was staying at her flat near the Fairholme Judo Club. I would come down from Hull for a week or two every now and then, and stay there, although she shared it with Dawn Netherwood – a regular member of the Yorkshire and Humberside team. Ann and I trained regularly and at first Ann found it a little difficult to keep up as I was a real fitness fanatic, but as she got more into the routine she coped very well. We laughed a lot as well, and occasionally went out –

though perhaps not often enough because by the time evening came round we were usually very tired after our extensive training sessions. Sometimes we would have a big eating binge to compensate – a typical response among many judo people, especially those, paradoxically, with a weight problem – and have to pay for it the following morning as we struggled our way through our three-mile run in our sweat gear.

With the one important international of the year out of the way, I could settle down and enjoy the smaller events, both at home and abroad, and they didn't go all my own way. I have never felt that I was unbeatable, otherwise I would have either cracked under the strain or appeared unbearably arrogant, and to lose once or twice a year is no bad thing.

I went on a judo holiday with Loretta – part of the prize for winning the World Championships – which was fun because it meant only a little judo and a lot of sun, and fortunately I tan easily. Shortly after my return, I fought in the British National Championships and won – beating none other than Sandy Fry in the final. Despite my international experience, she still managed to last the full time, forcing me to win on two kokas and a yuko. I was a member of the Yorkshire and Humberside team that won the national team championships again – we were on a run that was to take us to five titles in six years. And I won the Midland Area British Women's Closed gold medal.

Competition in America and Japan

Then came the Austrian Open, which I won by beating Valvano again, this time with three yukos, but I did not fight in the British Open because I was injured with slight tears to my hamstring. I only just recovered in time for a trip to America in November, though in the end it didn't turn out so well.

It was the only set-back in what would have otherwise been a clean record in 1983. I went with the squad to Colorado Springs for a week of altitude training at the main Olympic training camp. There I discovered that, whereas I love the sun, I do not react well to altitude. I hardly slept for five nights and my weight went down to 44 kilos. I looked like death warmed up, though I still tried to fit in all the training. I lost in the semi-final to Darlene Anaya, on a decision which upset me at the time, although in retrospect it was not important. In any case, we managed to fit in a week of sight-seeing afterwards which made the trip more than worth while. I was discovering that although the nomadic judo life can be testing, it does have its compensations.

This was followed by an even more exciting trip – my first visit to Japan. Although judo originated in Japan, the Japanese had taken a long time in developing women's judo. Women's judo did exist, but it had very few adherents in comparison with the millions who practised men's and children's judo, and those women judoka there were spent most of their time doing kata – formal practice – with very little randori. The Japanese did not hold their first National Championships for women until 1978!

So, it was not surprising that they made very little impression upon international judo, with the exception of the occasionally naturally talented fighters, such as the featherweight Kaori Yamaguchi. She had done very well to reach the World Championships final in 1980 and 1982, though she was not to win the title until 1984.

Understandably, the Japanese were keen to improve the competitive expertise of their women, and they approached the problem in a typical Japanese manner. They decided to hold five major international championships over five years, inviting – on an all-expenses-paid basis – winners of the gold and silver medals in the World Championships, and offering preferential rates for any other team members other countries cared to bring.

Although I didn't have an in-built sense of reverence towards Japanese judo the way that many Western men have – probably because I felt that in Britain women's judo was so much further ahead in competitive terms – I was very eager to go and see the home of judo. I didn't know what to expect, and the last thing was to be faced, on arrival at Fukuoka Airport on the southern island of Kyushu after a long and boring flight, with a mass of television cameras, photographers and reporters. The Japanese are into the media in a very big way.

Almost everything was a new experience. The hospitality was overwhelming, the organisation was superb, and what's more I felt very much at home because many of the people seemed so small. For a change I was able to talk to people – at least those who spoke English – without suffering a crick in the neck.

Everywhere we went we were followed by the television cameras and reporters. They all seemed to know who we were, and Loretta and I, as World Champions, had to become accustomed to signing autographs for everyone, from shopkeepers to people we met in the street. It was the first time I had truly experienced the feeling of being a celebrity outside the enclosed judo world. And the hospitality was so overwhelming it was bordering on embarrassing. Every time we saw ourselves on Japanese television we seemed to be eating!

The four of us who went from the British team – Loretta, Ann, Diane and myself – enjoyed all the details too, from the elegance of the hotel we stayed in, to the hakata, the Japanese night-time kimono that was laid out for us before going to bed. Of course, we couldn't quite forget that we were there to do judo, and even that first Fukuoka International Championships was hard – almost like a second World Championships. But both Loretta and I won, so it made the trip a near-perfect one.

There were other high points in 1983, though they were perhaps not so exotic. My old senior school, Bransholme High School, gave me an award for the best all-round pupil, though I had left three years earlier. It was really in recognition of my sporting achievements. And I was voted the Sportswoman of the Year by the *Yorkshire Post*, and the Northern Sportswoman of the Year by Vaux Breweries. The presentation was made the night before I was due to fly to Genoa for the European Championship, so it was all quite a rush. I attended the formal reception with my parents, made my first public speech, which went quite well, and in the early hours of the morning Diane (who also received an award) and I were escorted to an airstrip outside Sunderland and flown down to Heathrow on a small plane in order to join the team and travel on to Italy. For someone who was still only 19, this was living.

Into 1984

It was over the Christmas of 1983 that I began to appreciate how much responsibility goes with an unbeaten record at major international championships. I knew I wasn't infallible, and judo being such a dangerous juggling act, the slightest mistake can be punished severely. I had faltered momentarily in the United States in 1983 and I could see questions were being asked about whether my successful run was coming to an end. I didn't doubt myself, but I was acutely aware that whereas I enjoyed my first World Championships because I had everything to win, it would be different in Vienna in November 1984 because I had everything to lose. Nevertheless, it was not the personal satisfaction of being World Champion that I was concerned about – more the burden of the expectations of others. This is always the hardest burden to bear. This makes the records of sportsmen and women like Martina Navratilova, Ed Moses and judo's own example Yasuhiro Yamashita, the Japanese heavyweight undefeated for ten years, quite extraordinary. The toll it takes on the mental reserves of individuals such as these is far greater than the constant physical stress of maintaining peak fitness.

London Training

So, with the 1984 World Championships on the horizon, I resolved to come down and live in London in order to train full time with other members of the squad, enabling me to make the most of being in an environment of highly skilled companions. I was now nearly 21, however, and beyond the stage of sleeping on camp beds in the dojo. Fortunately, I was now in possession of a sports aid grant with a more realistic income, and my financial position was to be helped even more by the sponsorship of Hull City's telephone company, at the time the only independent telephone company in Britain. Conveniently, Dawn Netherwood moved out of the flat she shared with Ann Hughes near the Fairholme Judo Club in February, so I was able to move in.

It was an arrangement that worked very well, even when Diane started to come down regularly, staying at the flat so that we could train together. I knew it was the right decision in the long term, despite the difficulties I experienced at the first competition of the year.

My Challengers

I had been aware of an 18-year-old Scottish teenager, Anne-Marie Briody (later Mulholland). I had fought her in Scotland a year or so before and, if I remember correctly, strangled her unconscious – she wouldn't submit, which was very much in character. She was slightly smaller than me, but very strong and good with pick-ups, though she wasn't very skilled in other areas.

But she was a hard, scrappy fighter, probably a bit like me, 1981 vintage. We both went to the West German Open in Pirmasens, the site of the European Championships later in the year, and we met in the final. The way she took a quick grip, made an attack, and then let go was the complete opposite of my style – I like to be settled with my grip before launching an attack. We fought hard for five minutes, and when at the end there was no score, she won on a split decision.

I didn't feel it as a personal blow because the decision could have gone either way, but I did momentarily worry that it would affect my selection for the European Championships in March. In the event it did not, of course, and I was with the team that arrived back in Pirmasens, feeling in good form.

The preliminary rounds caused me few problems, and I was to meet one of my two French rivals again in the final, this time Fabienne Boffin. Boffin

The 1984 British Trials at Crystal Palace – grappling with Lena Strang of the Midlands in a contest I won with *juji-gatame*. I took the 52 kilos gold, with Strang third.

My *Kosoto-gai* in action.

was physically the opposite of Colignon. Where Colignon was skinny, tall and aggressive, Boffin was small and stocky, but both could throw well with big classical throws like *uchimata* and *osoto-gari*. They also both used the same tactics against me – taking a high grip at the back of my head, which I disliked. But I had learned to work against that grip, and in Pirmasens I threw Boffin in just over a minute, holding her down relatively easily.

It was a good event for the team, as Diane also won a gold, beating Gerda Winklbauer, the experienced Austrian, and there were three bronzes, from Anne Hughes, the young light heavyweight Teresa Hayden, and the heavyweight Sandra Bradshaw.

Winning my third European title was easier than some of the other events of the year. In the Swiss Open I met Anne-Marie Briody again in the final, and this time beat her on a yuko from *ouchi-gari*. We travelled abroad together again – though we didn't sit together on the plane – to the Dutch Open, where I really wanted to face Colignon once more before the World Championships in Vienna, even though I had an injured shoulder. We met in the semi-finals when I won with a yuko and learned more about her tactical approach which, I felt, would stand me in good stead later on. Briody again made the final on the other side of the draw, but I pulled out. By this time I had achieved the task I had set out to do, and my shoulder was not in a sufficiently good state to take on an opponent like Briody.

She was now training in London, and often at Fairholme Judo Club. I could see that she was watching me the whole time, working out ways to stop my major techniques, looking for any slight weakness in my stance or my grip. I didn't feel very threatened by her, but it was quite a wearing experience. I had to take a deep breath before I went on to the final of the British Open at Crystal Palace that year, having again had little trouble in the preliminaries but then having to get past Briody to retain my title.

I was up on attacks and feeling fairly secure when, about half-way through the contest, she attacked. I countered as I fell and, I felt, deserved the score, but she was given a waza-ari and knew enough about my techniques to be able to stop me levelling the score. It is one of the truths about judo that it is possible to stop a player producing a major technique if you know them very well, and, understandably, Briody went on to the defensive. I was forced to settle for the silver medal, which wasn't exactly what I had wanted with the World Championships just a month a way. But I was heartened by the fact that I had beaten all the foreign opposition I needed to that year, and underlined the fact by beating Colignon again in a home international against France, organised, rather stupidly, a few weeks before the World Championships. We were wiped out 5–2 with only Loretta and I winning, but once again I felt I could comfortably cope with Colignon.

My First World Title Defence

So, it was in a mood of optimism, though tinged with apprehension, that I arrived in Vienna with the British team for the third World Championships for women. I knew I was better prepared than I had ever been. For months I had paid particular attention to my groundwork, in an attempt to raise it to the standard of my tachiwaza. In fact, my groundwork wasn't bad at all – none of my main opponents at home or abroad were prepared to go to the ground with me – but I felt there were still areas which needed improvement. I had to be absolutely certain that once I was on an opponent's back, I could turn her into a hold, armlock or strangle, in the way that Neil Adams felt that, whenever he was on someone's back, an ippon was almost inevitable.

I worked ceaselessly at my turns, especially the roll into *sangaku-gatame,* and in randori took every opportunity to get on backs to start the technique. I worked out combinations into it, and combinations out of it, especially ending up in *kuzure-kame-shiho-gatame,* although my favourite hold at the time was *tate-shiho-gatame*.

I was to reap the rewards in Vienna. The pressure of walking on the mat as the title holder did get to me, because I didn't fight particularly well in the first round against Darlene Anaya, the American who had beaten me when I was suffering from altitude problems in Colorado Springs. I didn't find her particularly dangerous, but she was an awkward opponent. I was unable to score on her and had to rely on a decision.

The 1984 World Championships in Vienna – I used my low *tai-otoshi* to score waza-ari against Chodakowska of Poland, and went on to finish the contest a few seconds later with *tomoe-nage* for waza-ari.

Once through that first fight I relaxed. I had an enjoyable second round, throwing Anna Chodakowska of Poland for a series of part scores before catching her with a perfect *tomoe-nage* for ippon. Then my groundwork preparation began to pay off. I threw and then held down Anna-Maria Volvano of Italy and was ready to meet Marie-France Colignon in the final.

It was, of course, a repeat of the 1982 Paris final, but I was sure that on neutral territory I would be able to beat her with ippon. I received a minor shock when, after nearly a minute, she caught me with a footsweep for a koka, but I recovered more quickly from the shock than she did from her joy, for in almost the same action I caught her on the ground, and rolled her into *tate-shiho-gatame*, or at least a version of it where I sat high up on her body. Osaekomi was called, and I held on extremely tightly – there was no way she was going to escape. In his report, Philip Nicksan of *The Times* remarked that for nearly 30 seconds Colignon scarcely moved a muscle.

It was an important victory for me. For a start, it meant that I was the first Briton to have retained a world judo title. Neil Adams won his title in 1981 but lost the final in 1983, and Jane Bridge won her title in 1980 only to be supplanted by me.

Taking Stock

Retaining my world title also marked a technical turning point. I was now 21, a 3rd Dan and, I felt, I had achieved a standard of technical accomplishment that I could personally be pleased with. Every fighter meets difficult opponents where one style curiously negates another or 'bogy' opponents who, for some unaccountable reason, are always a struggle. But apart from these, I felt that I had achieved a balance between my fitness, strength, speed, throwing and groundwork techniques, and tactical awareness.

I was under no illusion that I could rest on my laurels, however. The unpredictability of judo was demonstrated by the accident suffered by Loretta Doyle, also defending her title, when she dislocated her shoulder against the American Robin Takemori. The middleweight Dawn Netherwood was the only other British girl to get a medal that year – she won a bronze.

But I also felt that a break of some kind would be a benefit. To take a year off was not a good idea – as Jane Bridge had found out. Instead, I decided to go up a weight, and try my luck in the 52 kilo category, the featherweight, a decision partly helped by the fact that Loretta was obviously going to be out for some time. I wasn't really searching for a head-on clash with her. Just weeks after the World Championships in Vienna, I was fighting in the British Trials at 52 kilos, although I was still barely 50 kilos. I won it without any real difficulty, confirming my decision to try the new weight in 1985.

But I came back down to 48 kilos for the last competition of the year, the Fukuoka Championships in Japan, where I went with Dawn and Diane Bell. It was an even more enjoyable time, for we managed to get in more sightseeing – we went to see the beautiful temples and tea gardens in Kyoto, one of the old Japanese capitals.

And both Diane and I won. The French sent Fabienne Boffin and Colignon and I had them both. I held Boffin down, this time using the *sangaku-gatame* roll I had practised for so many hours in Fairholme Judo Club, and then threw Colignon three times, with *tomoe-nage* for yuko, with *ouchi-gari* for waza-ari and with *te-guruma* for ippon. I was really enjoying myself. Diane, by the way, beat Winklbauer on points.

It was the end of an uneven year, with two defeats by Briody and the retention of my European and World titles, but I also felt I had come of judo age, so to speak.

The Los Angeles Olympics

Yet there was one other event which put my whole judo life into perspective. 1984 was, of course, the year of the Los Angeles Olympics. Women's judo had not been included, despite some last-ditch attempts to squeeze it into the programme, and it was evident that it was still regarded as a developing sport by the politicians. Along with the whole British judo world, I was shattered by the final of the light middleweights, where our own Neil Adams was quite unexpectedly thrown for ippon by the German Frank Wieneke when it looked as if he had the gold medal in his grasp.

I knew Neil well. Often, on Mondays I would go to practise at The Budokwai, in London, where he was the chief instructor, and there is no doubt that he is the most technically accomplished competitor Britain has ever produced. Neil took some time to acknowledge women's judo – even now there is a considerable amount of misogyny in British judo – but he has said some very complimentary things about my judo. I think that, in an unconscious way, I have been able to learn from his surprise defeat in the Olympics, and from some of the difficulties he had with his career when he retired.

6 New Challenges

I had been heartened by the surprisingly easy way in which I managed to make the domestic transition to under 52 kilos, even though I was really nowhere near the limit, and I was looking forward to seeing what it was like abroad. Over Christmas 1984 I could eat and drink to my heart's content, knowing that the task now was to put on weight, not take it off. I needed quality weight, however, so I started on a reworked weights programme.

It was a refreshing and relaxing time in a strange way because the pressure was off. All the main points of the discussions I had had with Roy about 1985, which resulted in my decision to try the featherweight category, seemed to be correct. I expressed them in an interview with Hull's *Daily Mail*, which, by the way, had catalogued my career faithfully from my very early days.

'When I retained the world title, it was a question of ''where do I go from here'' '? I said in the interview a week after Vienna. 'I have been competing at bantamweight for six years and I feel I need a new challenge.'

I said that I would have to learn to alter my skills slightly to operate at the higher weight category, but not as much as others might expect. 'I might be a bit fast for them, which will cause a few problems. I think I will shock a few.'

And, I am glad to say, I did. After a couple of months of intensive weight training, I went into the West German Open, though I was still only 50 kilos because I didn't want to stop running which I enjoyed. I won my first three fights with maximum points, then beat my French opponent with a yuko, and finally gained a points victory over Edith Hrovat, the experienced Austrian Champion, and one of my main likely rivals in this new weight.

European Championships in Landskrona

I returned to Hull quite optimistic about the forthcoming European Championships in Landskrona, Sweden. But the optimism turned out to be misplaced. While I beat Hrovat again in the first round of the Europeans, I then met Pascale Doger of France, who had won bronze medals in two World Championships. I knew she used to struggle with her weight, and by the time we actualy met I reckoned her weight must have shot up to 55 kilos, about five kilos more than me. She felt very strong and heavy, and I felt very unstable. She scored a waza-ari with a footsweep early on in the fight. I managed to get a koka back, but couldn't level the match.

I came back in the *repêchage* to win a bronze, but I knew then that I was just not a featherweight. Roy asked me if I was upset, and I said calmly that I wasn't because it wasn't my best weight category, but it was worth the try.

If there was any doubt in my mind, it was resolved by seeing Anne-Marie Briody winning a bronze, with Colignon taking the title. However many difficulties I may have had with the Scots girl, I knew that my international place was on top of the under 48 kilo rostrum.

Britain still came away with a gold medal from the Europeans that year, this time through the heavyweight Sandra Bradshaw, one of the most introverted members of the team but a player with superb stability and a spectacular hip throw. Though much smaller than most of her opponents, she could really throw them for ippon once she got them on her hips.

When I came back from Sweden, I had decided I was coming back down to 48 kilos. I fought in the Dutch Open, but I was not really in good mental shape because my mother had been seriously ill. Quite uncharacteristically, I was strangled by an Austrian girl. I was well up on knock-down scores when we went to the ground about three-quarters of the way through the contest. She was on her back and I was between her legs beginning an attacking movement, when I suddenly felt a strangle coming on. I started to stand up to initiate a 'break' call from the referee, but this made the strangle come on even more severely. Once again, however, I understood the technical mistake I had made, and accepted the defeat as a valuable lesson, ignoring the surprised looks of others who could only see that in one year I had now been defeated twice at two weight categories.

European Team Event

Up to this point, I had been relatively fortunate with injuries, suffering remarkably few problems. But the years of turning at speed, which traditionally wreaks havoc with the knees of judo players, finally caught up with me, and I was forced to rest and undergo an operation. My ligaments had been badly stretched, and if I was to have a reasonable chance of retaining my world title in 1986, I had to have this sorted out now.

So I missed the British Open that year, but was back in time to fight in the European Team Championships in Belgium. I won all my fights, but we were just beaten by France in the preliminaries and had to settle for a bronze. It is clear that the interest in team events internationally is diminishing, because the sports world seems only interested in individual medals, except for the big team games. This is a pity because often team events can be more exciting than individual championships, with very different tactics playing an important role. And often the highly ranked players are turned over by comparatively lowly opponents. Some of my most enjoyable judo competitions have been team events, both for Yorkshire and Humberside, and for Britain.

Time to Relax

The ease of pressure in 1985 allowed me to enjoy myself more in other ways. Judo being such an enclosed world, it was not surprising that I had formed a close friendship with Roy Stone, one of the boys at the Fairholme Judo Club. He was a few years younger than me, but I liked him a lot. We started going out in September 1984, when he had finished his A levels and was starting to train full time – he was a very promising under 71 kilo player. We used to train together during the day. At first he had quite a problem keeping up with my running, although he eventually got into the flow of it. We would then go into the dojo and he would do weights while I did circuits. Both being quite volatile, we had a few arguments, but remained together until April 1986, which was quite a long time for me – I think I take quite a lot of pleasing. And, much to my surprise, we didn't talk a lot about judo when we were together.

It was in the summer of 1985 that I was to have my first contact with the playwright John Godber, opening a totally unexpected chapter in my life. Although I knew of the Hull Truck Theatre Company – it had the reputation of being one of the best small theatre companies of its kind in the country – I had never been to see it. In fact, I had never seen a live play at all. It just wasn't the kind of thing that I thought of doing. Out of the blue, one July afternoon, I had a call from John Godber, the resident writer at the Hull Truck Theatre Company, who had already won some top theatre awards for a play about rugby league called *Up and Under*. He said he wanted to see me because he was interested in writing a play about judo, based on myself. The way he explained it later in the press was that he had already written about the most important sport in Hull – rugby league – and now he wanted to write about the leading sports personality, which was me.

I was delighted because I could see that it would help to put judo on the map. It is still regarded as a minority sport and, despite the success that British judo players have, does not get the recognition it deserves. We met after a session at the Kingston Judo Club and went for a drink with my father and Barry Nettleton, the theatre administrator. I was surprised by John Godber, because he is a very big man – well over six feet tall and with a very big build. And he was surprised by how small I was – just five feet. 'I didn't know you were so small – you look much bigger on TV,' he said honestly.

He admitted that he didn't know anything about judo, and thought that the best idea was to have a go himself – he was that sort of man. He came down to the club a couple of nights later and was surprised that although he was a very big man who could push heavy weights, he was quite easily held down by a much smaller Dan grade. John tells how the Dan grade asked him how long he had been doing judo, and John replied: 'About 20 seconds – the time you have been holding me down.'

Afterwards we went to a restaurant, and John said he was still just looking at the possibilities, but that he would have no difficulties at all in putting judo on stage. He even asked me if I would like to appear in it, but I said that it would mean too much time away from competition which was not advisable, particularly with the 1986 World Championships now only a year away. I was quite tempted, however, to have a go at acting.

I didn't hear anything from John for some time after that, and I began to think that nothing would come of it. What I didn't know was that the play itself, and plans for the first production, had progressed rapidly, and by the autumn there were actors and actresses preparing to learn judo in clubs up and down the country in order to be able to play their parts. Liza Sandovy was learning judo at The Budokwai in London, and Jane Thornton was learning her judo at my own club in Hull. John phoned me in November and came to borrow books and videos. What he wanted to do was not to give a straight account of my life, but to draw on various aspects to create a drama showing the many different parts of judo – from the competitive world to its ability to change a person's whole approach to life.

Third Victory in Japan

The end of 1985 brought, as usual, the Fukuoka International Championships. Once again, I found myself on that long plane trip, with a short stop at Anchorage. We arrived in Fukuoka to face a barrage of television men, as always, and went to the same hotel. Everything was exactly the same as before – to an extraordinary extent. The rooms, the presents, the timetable, the celebrations – the Japanese reproduced every tiny detail year after year. I obviously fell into the same pattern, because the result was exactly the same as the last year. I beat Fabienne Boffin in the semi-finals with ippon again, this time throwing her with *tomoe-nage*, and then threw Colignon for ippon in the final with *te-guruma*. I was pleased because, with no World Championships that year, this was really the top international event, and after a less than successful year from a competitive point of view, it confirmed that I was still on top.

I came back from Japan still quite hungry for judo and training. I was aware that 1986 was going to be an important year, with the Europeans and the World Championships, and the play which was now scheduled to tour the country, and possibly go on television. I decided to train lightly through Christmas. I ran regularly, and did other fitness work, so I felt in good shape when I returned to London on 1 January to be ready for the first judo session of the year at the Fairholme Judo Club on 2 January.

7 Disaster and Triumph

Scheduled to be one of my busiest competitive years, at least in terms of top international events, 1986 promised the European Championships, the Commonwealth Games, where judo was included for the first time, the World Championships, and finally the Fukuoka Championships again. Even in those first two days of January, I could feel the pressure beginning to build. There was no reason why, with a good training programme, I should not go through all those events and retain the major titles, for I still felt that I had the edge, both technically and physically, on all my rivals.

But rationality is little defence against the kind of pressure that exists when you are the one everyone wants to beat. The difference between the people at the very top in any sport is always tiny. My *tomoe-nage*, and the way I closed down my opponents' options in groundwork, may have allowed me a little lead, but really the difference is best measured on a mental level. What was once described as my 'fierce mental determination' coupled with the ability to produce my best when under the greatest stress, was probably what enabled me to win the world title, and then retain it. There was more pressure in 1984 than 1982, and for 1986 I knew that the level of pressure would be even greater.

When I look back over my career, I find that, almost by accident, my body, or circumstances, have an extraordinary ability to find the right time and the right means of putting into operation a safety valve, like the release valve on a pressure cooker. This safety valve effect came into operation in those small competitions where I have made mistakes and lost. Thus, being thrown for ippon by Colignon a couple of months before my first World Championships put me on course for the first world title. Losses against Anne-Marie Briody showed everyone something that I knew well – that I was only human, and certainly not omnipotent, even on my home territory. There are so many unpredictable factors in judo. Not only can you be beaten soundly, but you can lose for many other reasons, including a referee's mistake (they too are human) and sheer bad luck.

My little sortie into the 52 kilo category gave me the break I desperately needed while maintaining my involvement in judo. So I was determined not to be put off by any small setbacks that I would encounter in my preparations for the main 1986 programme. But I was certainly not ready for what actually happened, in what was to be my most extraordinary year.

I was expecting to follow much the same procedure of living in the flat with Ann and being joined by Diane for the training sessions when she came down. Three was definitely not a crowd for us. We were still getting on very well and we had a lot of fun together. I think my parents had resigned themselves to the fact that I would be more or less based in London from now on. I was getting an Elite Grant, on much the same basis as Cram and Coe, and was therefore financially quite independent, with my own car, and my bike – I still cycled for enjoyment as much as fitness.

Unlike many sports, it is crucial to have good and regular training partners in judo. While much of the fitness work can be done alone – although solitary training is always an austere business – the judo work which must be the central part of a preparation programme requires a partner, and ideally an equally skilled partner, not just anybody.

Ann, Diane and I seemed to make up a perfect group, for our fitness levels and our awareness of judo training programmes were well matched. Off the mat, too, our personalities seemed to blend and on foreign trips, it was always we who started the ball rolling as far as the post-competition release was concerned, which generally meant some uninhibited drinking.

My relationship with Roy Inman had settled too. I was no longer the painfully shy girl walking in awe of him, but in a fast-moving banter I began to give as good as I got. There was no doubt in my mind that I needed him, for he is the greatest women's judo coach in the world, and despite my two world titles, I didn't think I could simply go on winning on my own.

Injured

Despite being quite a large man – over 90 kilos – Roy was a very good practice partner, being very skilful and knowing exactly how much strength to use when doing randori with a woman of my size. On 2 January, I set off for the Fairholme Judo Club, looking forward to a randori after the Christmas break – a judo player begins to feel withdrawal symptoms after too long away from a 'good pull'. The session had been going for about 45 minutes when I went on with Roy. We were having our normal fast interchange when he suddenly caught me with a superbly-timed *uchimata*. As I landed, my foot hit the mat from the heel and I heard an ominous crack. It was an absolutely clean *uchimata* throw – he didn't land on me or anything like that – but I just landed awkwardly. The pain was very bad and I burst into tears – and it takes a lot of pain to make me cry. Roy was panicking and said: 'Is it your knee?' which is the first consideration of a judo player, for knee injuries are often the worst. I replied: 'No, it's my foot, but don't touch it!'

Even at this stage it had begun to swell and a large lump developed on the inside of my foot near the arch. Roy was convinced it was a sprain, or, more to the point, he was hoping it was just a sprain. I tried standing, but it was no good – I could not put any weight on the foot. I was convinced then that I had broken something, and Roy carried me off the mat and put me in the sauna to get some heat on the foot. I then put my foot in a bowl of ice – using the snow from outside because it had been snowing hard. It was now 10.15 p.m., and I decided to go to the hospital to have it checked out – it was always better to be safe than sorry.

Ann Hughes kindly drove me to Ashford Hospital. I told the hospital reception that I had fallen downstairs because I thought that perhaps I would be seen quicker – many hospitals have a curious attitude towards sports injuries; they feel they are almost self-inflicted and can be quite unconcerned.

The doctor took one look at the foot and sent me to X-ray, which confirmed a fractured cuniform, one of the arch bones in the foot. The doctor then asked me if I was sure that I fell downstairs, as it was unusual to find the foot crushed like this, so I told him the truth. He then said that he had some good news and some bad news. The bad news was that I had a bad fracture of the right foot; and the good news was that he could set it slightly to ease most of the pain.

I arrived home at 1.30p.m., but even with painkillers I could not sleep. My toes were black and blue, but I was now crying, more because I was upset than because of the pain. Roy telephoned me early that morning and said that he was praying it was not broken. I told him I had a plaster right up to my knee, and that it was a break. He was extremely upset, and was almost too frightened to ask how long the plaster would have to stay on. He was very concerned.

I went back to hospital that day to have the plaster reset and a stronger cast put on. I was now very worried, not so much because of the fracture itself but because I did not know whether I would be ready to fight in the European Championships which were just eleven weeks away, and which, ironically, were to be held for the first time in London.

I telephoned my parents to tell them the bad news and they were very upset as they knew my total commitment to my judo and my career. I told them that the doctor had said I might be in plaster for the whole of those eleven weeks, but that he had agreed to give me an appointment five weeks ahead to see how it was going. As I went home on crutches, I became very depressed because for the first time I began to think that this may mean the end of my career. I kept thinking about what the doctor had said: that although I was an athlete, my bones would take just as long to heal as everyone else's, and perhaps even longer because I had to be able to perform complex movements at speed, while other people simply had to walk.

After a few more days, the cast came off again, and a permanent cast was put on. I went home to stay with my parents, as I knew I would be hell to live with over those next weeks. The problem was that I didn't know what I was going to do with myself after being so active for so many years. It was like being locked in a small room. Although I found I could concentrate for hours running, or doing judo training, or when I was working for something, my concentration on all other things was minimal, largely because I wasn't really interested in what I was doing. Even now, I can only watch television for a short time before my attention wanders.

Convalescing with Hull Truck Theatre Company

But I had to find something, and my hobbies over this period increased. I always loved sewing, and I made various tapestry pictures; my mother taught me to knit too, which was not easy. Although neither my mother nor my father really knew what to do with my boredom, they did understand my feelings which was very important to me at this time.

Then the play came to my rescue. I had been in plaster for about two weeks when John Godber got back in touch with me, and invited me to go and help with the judo side of the play. It was a godsend. Working on the play was not only a new experience, but it took my mind off things a little. I went to the theatre for about two weeks, from 9 a.m. to 6 p.m., and soon stopped feeling sorry for myself. I was coaching the actors and actresses in the play, even with my leg in plaster. The play was actually set in an old judo club – just like Kingston Judo Club used to be before it moved to its new premises in the community centre. There was quite a lot of actual judo in the play, and if it had been rather amateurish it would have dragged the whole drama down with it. It was vital that we got the judo to an acceptable standard, and I must say I was surprised how well the players coped, because judo is not easy.

The play centred on the story of two girls who arrive at a judo club to learn some kung fu self-defence. They have no idea what judo is all about, and at first treat it like a big joke. But the magic of judo catches the imagination of one of the girls, and as the play develops, the progress of the girls is

With John Godber (left) and Barry Nettleton, Administrator of the Hull Truck Theatre Company.

contrasted. One just takes the normal route of life, with discos and boyfriends, eventually ending up pregnant; while the other girl changes and learns the enriching feeling of a discipline, finally getting her black belt.

There are sub-plots too, but the essence of the story was the development of the character of that girl – told with great humour and fun and some raw images and words that are very true to life. John Godber had used bits of my life to build up various characters – one of the dramatic highlights is the successful use of *tomoe-nage* by the heroine. And he had also drawn on some of the best stories from the Kingston Judo Club, one of which I actually saw happen.

We were in the old school, which was in a very bad state, and a stranger came on to the mat to try judo. We had new people all the time so this was nothing special. But after half an hour or so, when we were doing some throwing. I suddenly saw a black shaggy thing shoot across the mat. We all stopped because we though it was a big black rat – a real possibility in such an old building – but it turned out to be this stranger's toupee. He didn't come back.

The play created a lot of interest. There were large features in major newspapers like *The Times* and *The Guardian* in time for the opening of the play in Hull's Spring Street Theatre in February. It was another marvellous diversion for me, and I was photographed throwing John Godber, though diplomatically the photo only showed our heads and top halfs – World Champion I may be, but it would be the devil's own job to throw a six-foot four, 18-stone man with one leg in a plaster cast up to my knee. However, no doubt, someone, somewhere believed it was possible!

By this time John Godber was a very successful playwright, with not only *Up and Under* highly regarded, but *Up and Under II*, and *Bouncers*, a very funny play about being on the doors of clubs in the North-east. So *Blood, Sweat and Tears*, inspired by Karen Briggs, World Judo Champion, created a lot of interest, and the Hull Truck Theatre Company was booked not only to take it to London, but also right around the country – a year of almost solid touring. It was even scheduled to be in Edinburgh in the summer at the time of the Commonwealth Games.

I enjoyed the play very much. I saw it quite a few times, in Hull and in London, and then on television when it was screened. But I was, by now, counting the days, as it got closer to my appointment with the hospital and the plaster cast being taken off. Throughout this period, Roy Inman had kept on telephoning me to ask how I was, which was typically thoughtful of him – but he could tell from my voice that I was not my normal self. I also wondered whether he was beginning to think that I was enjoying myself in the theatre world so much that I wouldn't get back to competition at all.

Training through my Injury

Even when I was at home with my leg in plaster, I did not neglect my training. I did various exercises to keep my upper body, my arms and my left leg in trim, because I knew that my right foot was deteriorating, being completely isolated. I worked out a hard hour's training every day which covered as much ground as I possibly could, although I did have some trouble finding ways of working my cardio-vascular system, as I could neither run nor swim.

I went back to Ashford Hospital on 8 February with the team doctor, Ken

Kingsbury. A word must be said about Dr Kingsbury here, for he is one of the most experienced judo doctors in the world, having looked after generations of British team members, and often finds himself, during international competitions, called on for consultation by other teams.

I had an X-ray, and although the doctor was not very impressed, I said that the plaster had to come off if I was to have any chance of competing in the European Championships in March, which was just weeks away. As usual, Dr Kingsbury, the judo doctor, was with me at the time and persuaded his colleague to allow the plaster to be taken off. He knew how my mind worked: had the European Championships been anywhere else but London, the plaster would have stayed so that the natural healing process could have taken its course. But if it was humanly possible, I had to be on that Crystal Palace mat.

Now at last I could start to work – and there was no more time for tapestry. I had intensive physiotherapy at New Victoria Hospital for almost six weeks, and Rosemary Lillie, the team physiotherapist who has travelled to competitions with us on numerous occasions, did a brilliant job getting me to walk again. It was quite painful, and sometimes I wished that I could have the plaster cast back on – until I remembered the Europeans.

I began swimming a lot. I would swim for nearly two miles, and cycle 25 miles to and from physiotherapy every day, which was more or less my training schedule for the Europeans. At the hospital, I had more X-rays which revealed that ten days before the competition, the bone was still fractured, and that after the competition I would probably need an operation to realign it in the foot.

Throughout this time, Roy Stone stayed with me. I wasn't getting on very well with the girls in the squad. Very often long injuries cause difficulties in relationships because they interfere with the work that needs to be done. It is difficult for both sides – for the healthy who want to work at full stretch and find it difficult to go carefully or slowly; and for the injured who needs to be extra careful, and is perhaps hypersensitive. The personal attention Roy gave me during those two weeks or so made an enormous difference to the way I felt mentally as well as to my physical preparation.

It was just ten days before the event that I stepped on a judo mat. I wore a running shoe on my bad foot with a sock over it because I had problems walking in my bare feet – my arch bones needed support. I did a few throws and groundwork with the juniors and began to wonder whether it was realistic for me to consider competing – after all, I would be going on with the best women in the world with less than five hours of mat practice and only one randori. I couldn't even run.

European Championships in London

I felt very uneasy as I travelled with the team to the Holiday Inn near Crystal Palace the night before. Roy Inman was very helpful in trying to console me and talked to me for over two hours that evening after I weighed in. It wasn't helped by the fact that I had one of the hardest possible draws – I did not even get the luck of a bye.

I began the morning of the event with a visit from Dr Kingsbury who gave me a pain-killing injection right into the foot. It was then heavily strapped, but even with that I walked with a noticeable limp. I had no idea what was going to happen – what my fitness would be like, what my judo was going to be like, and whether my foot was going to be able to stand up to the strain of top competition.

I warmed up, strangely enough, with Ann, even though we had been barely speaking to each other. We were fighting on the same day, and I remember saying on the warm-up mat: 'Come on, Ann – we have not been seeing eye to eye, but we shouldn't let it affect our judo. We both need to win.' So we warmed up together. Ann was unusually nervous, and I tried to help.

I certainly felt uneasy as I stepped on the mat in my first fight against Anna Maria Valvano (Italy), whom I had beaten in the final of the European Championships in 1983. It became painfully evident when she footswept me at the beginning for a koka. But it seemed to shake the dust from my eyes. I suddenly realised where I was and what I was trying to do. And I forgot about my foot. I began moving around with some of my old fluency, and spun in for my *tomoe-nage*. Over the top the Italian went, for an ippon score. It was just the start I needed.

Almuth Leitgeb proved a slightly more testy opponent. I knocked her down with an *ouchi-gari*, a *tomoe-nage* and a *tai-otoshi*, but as she huddled into a defensive posture on the ground, I went into my *sangaku* turning routine and held her down in *kame-shiho-gatame*, which took the pressure off my foot.

It was holding out quite well but now I faced potentially the toughest opponent, Fabienne Boffin of France. I felt that I wouldn't catch her with *tomoe-nage* as I had done in the Fukuoka Championships in December, and was thinking of *te-guruma* as I prepared for the fight. Curiously, just as I was about to walk on the mat, Roy came up to me and mentioned *te-guruma* quietly to me. It is strange how coach and player can become almost telepathic at instances like these.

And right at the beginning of the fight, as soon as Boffin stepped in for the inevitable *uchimata*, I stepped around it, picked her up and threw her with *te-guruma*. It very nearly finished the fight there and then – but a waza-ari was awarded rather than the ippon.

I went back into the attack, trying everything I knew, from *tai-otoshi* to *tomoe-nage* to another *te-guruma*, but I just lacked that edge. It was as if I had produced my best right at the start of the fight – which was the only time I could have done it. In one exchange, I hurt my foot, and began limping, but as the seconds ticked away, I felt I was safely into the final.

There was a long wait for the final, of course. I talked with my team-mates – Diane had also won through to her final, and Ann was fighting for a bronze medal. Sandra Bradshaw, the heavyweight, was also in the final, hoping to win the title for a second time running.

My first ippon of the day in the 1986 European Championships – one of my best *tomoe-nages*.

I could see the sense of relief on Roy's face. I hadn't realised, until then, that the last few weeks had been agony for him, for although he knew that the injury was a total accident, he had felt the pressure and the uncertainty too. It showed me how caring he really was. My father, too, was relieved that I had come through to the final relatively unscathed. He had come down from Hull for the competition with my sister Anita who was watching me compete at a top championship for the first time. My mother was again very ill and unable to travel.

I had another pain-killing injection before I went on because the foot had started to swell quite badly, and I had limped off the mat after the semi-final. But I was actually looking forward to the final itself – even in those circumstances I didn't feel that Loly Verguillas of Spain was a real threat, although I knew from experience that over-confidence is one of the great dangers in judo.

In the event, I had a ball. She was evidently unnerved by the occasion and the place, and kept going over for a succession of minor scores. My first *tai-otoshi* attempt didn't score, but that was about the only one that did not. I threw her with *tomoe-nage* for a koka, an *ouchi-gari* for yuko, a left hip throw for yuko (though it was first scored for waza-ari). But I couldn't seem to nail her for the ippon. Then, manoeuvring near the middle of the mat, I suddenly spun in for a *tomoe-nage*. Over the top went Señorita Verguillas – cleanly on to her back. It was one of the most satisfying moments of my life.

For some unaccountable reason I had fought as well as I had ever done, despite the lack of training and the half-healed injury – or perhaps because of them. This is the unpredictable nature of sport in general, and judo in particular. I still felt the pressure, although the injury could have acted as a release from the overwhelming expectation of the British judo world for a win on home ground. Whatever the case, it seemed that something allowed the technique that was within me after years of hard work to come out of its own accord. When I watch the videos, I can only remark that my performance on that day was technically one of the best.

And I was delighted to find that television was there in force. Only rarely does television attend judo competitions in Britain, because the medium is so concerned with what they call the major sports. But this time the BBC were preparing a 20-minute programme on me, involving interviews, an excerpt from *Blood, Sweat and Tears*, and the competition.

The day was even better because Diane won her second gold medal and Ann her bronze. The two had swapped weight categories, with Diane going up to light middleweight and Ann dropping to lightweight after the 1984 World Championships. Here, in their first major international, and on their home ground, they were demonstrating that the decision was the correct one. Sadly, Sandra Bradshaw lost her final against Beata Maksymow of Poland, and then retired, despite the relative proximity of the World Championships.

The following day, my foot had swollen up badly – but I didn't expect it to do anything else after the rigours of a European Championship. I went back to the surgeons, and they were puzzled as to how I broke the bone in the first place. They said it was almost impossible to do it without breaking many of the other bones in my foot. It was like a balloon, and clearly needed a rest.

Commonwealth Games in Edinburgh

In April, I moved out of the flat and back to Hull once more. I saw more surgeons – seeking different opinions after one foot specialist told me to pull out of all competitions for the rest of the year – and they told me first to rest it. When rest seemed to make no difference, they decided that perhaps a further operation to shave a splinter off the bone would be necessary. I wanted to be back in time for the Commonwealth Games in July, but my eyes were really on the retention of my world title in November.

Manipulation was tried, and eventually the foot seemed to heal itself on its own, although when I arrived in Edinburgh for the Commonwealth Games in July, it still had to be heavily strapped. Strictly speaking, judo was classed as a demonstration event, and was therefore not formally part of the main games. But in the event, it turned out to be one of the most popular –

Throwing Anne-Marie Mulholland of Scotland in the 1986 Commonwealth Games with *tomoe-nage* for waza-ari.

in terms of audience – and spectacular of all events. It drew a huge entry from throughout the Commonwealth, with two fighters allowed in each weight category, and the men and women fought on the same day – the first time this was to happen in a major international, although now it is standard practice.

As luck would have it, I drew Anne-Marie Briody – now fighting for Scotland under her married name of Mulholland – for my very first fight. There was no doubt that she represented my strongest opponent, and if a sensible seeding system existed, we should have been drawn on opposing sides, so that we would meet in the final. In the end, we did both.

The competition was run with pools in the first round, the top two from each pool going through to the knockout rounds. In the first fight, I took a calculated gamble. I used only *tai-otoshi*, *ouchi-gari* and *te-guruma*, specifically avoiding the *tomoe-nage* which she knew so well. I didn't score, but I was well ahead on attacks by the time the bell went. I sailed through the rest of the fights to meet her again in the final – which didn't really surprise me. Now, I changed tactics. As soon as I gripped up, and started to move, I turned in for *tomoe-nage*, and over she went for waza-ari. It was a sweet moment. I managed another knock-down, although the final ippon eluded me, but it was enough.

I was pleased not only to win the first games, but also to be awarded a glass goblet for the most stylish player in the women's event. In fact, the strength of the British women's team was shown by the fact that each of the categories was won by a Briton.

With my foot now completely healed, I was able to go back into the training and competition programme. I had spent the week prior to the Commonwealth Games in Nice, on a course with Roy and Jane Bridge – who was now helping Roy with the women's team – and I knew that I was ready to undertake serious work again.

Back to London

I started in August, but without my realising it, the stress of the coming event was beginning to make itself felt. While I had my injured foot and had moved back to Hull, Ann and Diane had grown closer together, and after the Europeans I found that I didn't get on with them so well. I had moved my things out of the flat and back to Hull, but at the same time Roy mentioned the possibility of moving into another flat he had hired for the use of various members of the women's squad who came to train with him from time to time. This was an ideal solution, for it gave me an independent base in London while allowing me to be a free agent – coming and going to Hull as I pleased – without disrupting Ann and Diane. I was 23 now, and I felt I wanted to be more independent, rather than living with a group of girls all the time.

So in August of 1986 I came back down to London to the flat, and joined in with the training sessions. Relationships with Ann were a little strained, but we knew that we had at least to be able to train together – that is part and parcel of being a member of a women's squad. I began working with other partners, including Jackie Johnson, a young but talented girl who had started to train full time, and was very keen; and Sharon Rendle, my old friend and occasional rival from Yorkshire and Humberside, who was now really contending for the top place in the under 52 kilo category, the light heavyweights, where Loretta Doyle was no longer the dominating force she had been. I also trained with Roy's son, Peter Inman, who was a perfect partner at the time – a skilful teenager who was then only a little taller than myself.

And the tone of my life changed. I was enjoying having a slightly broader social life than normally is the case with full-time judo athletes who have to train during the day and do their randori at night. Judo players can be very lonely people and become hermits if they are not careful, but Sharon, who is very gregarious, used to make me go out for drinks. I slowly began to realise that perhaps this varied life would enable me to go on longer in my judo career, so long as I kept a happy medium.

Austrian Open

In September I went to the Austrian Open and won comfortably. It was a memorable occasion for me for another reason. Ann and I decided to put our differences aside and we celebrated it with a drink after the competition, but before the formal reception that always ends these affairs. One drink led to another, and by the time the reception started, I am afraid Ann and I were in no fit state to attend it. It was the first one I had ever missed, and I felt a little bad, but there was nothing I could do. Neither of us could stand all that well, and Roy, understandably, would not risk letting us go looking like that. I remember somebody holding Ann up, as she could not stand at all, and I then remember being rather noisy and insisting that I was perfectly capable of going to the reception. Roy was angry, but in his way understood, and sat with Ann and I for much of the night to make sure I didn't do anything stupid. The job of the team manager does not begin and end on the judo mat or in the fitness room. I now make a conscious effort to get to the official receptions.

British Open

I was quite pleased with the preparations for the World Championships which were being held in Maastricht, Holland. I had just one more tournament before the big day – the British Open in October. I felt reasonably confident and was slightly angered when an awkward but otherwise not dangerous Polish fighter kicked my knee severely in the first fight. I won, but had to have the knee strapped up in order to go on. In fact Roy was so concerned about my condition for the forthcoming World Championships that he told me to withdraw, but as I had the competitive bit between my teeth, I wasn't going to stop now. In any case, I had been injured before most of my British Open competitions, so this was nothing new.

I hobbled through three other fights, doing a professional rather than a spectacular job, and really only turned on the fireworks in the final against Friedrich of West Germany. I threw her with an odd but effective combination of *tai-otoshi* and *te-guruma*, and then rolled her into *kame-shiho-gatame* for ippon. Roy did not congratulate me afterwards – I think he was angry at my decision to continue because further injury could have jeopardised the defence of my world title.

In the same competition, my training partner Sharon Rendle sealed her ticket to the World Championships by beating Loretta Doyle, throwing her twice.

The 1986 British Open at Crystal Palace – forcing my opponent to the ground in the final.

Second World Title Defence

And so on to the World Championships. The pressure was greater than I have ever felt before, for a number of reasons. First of all, it must be remembered that throughout my competitive career, women's judo had been improving generally in leaps and bounds, whereas men's judo has remained relatively static in terms of the international technical level. I had managed constantly to improve my own judo, and at times, perhaps, I was improving at a faster rate than most of my competitors. But I knew from the experience of the international events I had attended that the gap was getting closer and closer. Each month, it seemed, the level of skill, fitness, tactical awareness and sheer strength of the average international woman player improved.

It was a year since I had fought any of the top Eastern women, and they were rather unknown quantities. The Chinese had already showed that they could produce some extremely good judo girls, drawing on their massive population and enthusiasm for the Chinese martial arts and gymnastics. The Americans had already proved that they could produce some tough opponents. And what about the traditionally strong judo nations who had come late to women's judo, such as the Russians, the Koreans and the Japanese? Would they, at last, be equal to their men?

Then again, there was the new organisation, which meant that the event was now spread over three days, with my weight category coming on the very last day. My preparation was good. For a change, I was without injury as I stepped on the mat – I even felt slightly odd because of it. And my

Throwing Roy Inman, just before the 1986 World Championships.

weight had dropped to 45 kilos again, partly through nerves and partly because I was still running, as it helps to keep my nerves in check. In the event I had a relatively easy draw, with a bye in the first round, although, frankly, I could have done with another warm-up fight.

We stayed in a hotel away from the main judo hotel for a change because it was cheaper, and we had a lot of supporters whom we wanted to see. I had difficulty in sleeping, and for almost a week I seemed to have a permanent headache. I had a slight graze on my right elbow from a burn I had stupidly sustained in a sauna, but I could feel the tension getting to me and sapping my strength in a way that it had never done before. The Belgian light heavyweight Ingrid Berghmans knew what the tension was all about – she had won the World open title three times in a row, and here she was defending it on her home ground. Brigitte Deydier, the French middleweight, also knew what it was like, for she had won her weight category twice in a row and was bound to draw a string of supporters from across the border.

The first day's competition went without a medal for Britain. The second day produced a remarkable result, with both Ann Hughes and Diane Bell winning their categories – a marvellous double for the training partners; and especially for Diane, who had dislocated her thumb in the first round, but snapped it back into place and went on to win. She beat her French opponent, Celine Geraud, in the final with a koka from *ouchi-gari*, scored in the last two seconds of the fight.

In addition, Sharon had fought very well, winning a bronze and showing herself more than capable of reaching a world final. Of course, with my fights coming the next day, I couldn't celebrate with them, but kept away

Showing the stress of judo competition . . .

from the drinking and singing, trying to find a quiet place somewhere in order to think and prepare myself mentally.

The Eastern countries had produced some excellent players in the other weights, and I didn't know much about my opponents – while I knew that they would have had no difficulty in watching me on video, and developing ploys to negate my strong moves and exploit my weaknesses.

By the time I stepped on the mat on the third day, I was strung up tight like a bow, not helped by the fact that while my mother and sister were there, my father was in hospital at home having an operation on his back. I knew that I was fit, but at first I just couldn't settle. Nevertheless I took hold of my first opponent, Eira Helenius of Finland, and immediately scored a yuko from *tai-otoshi*. I then let her stand up, because I knew I needed more time on the mat, under the glare of the lights and the crowd, to prepare myself for the tougher competition that was to come. Once again, I left *tome-nage* alone for a little. I scored another yuko with *tai-otoshi* and then felt I couldn't play around any longer – after all, this was the World Championships. So I rolled her over and held her down in *kame-shiho-gatame*. The fight was all over in under a minute.

I had watched my next opponent, Ju Ping Chou from Taipei carefully. Though Taipei is not known as a strong judo nation, this girl had thrown two good ippons in her first two rounds, and I knew she could not be treated lightly. I took hold cautiously, and just felt her movement for a few moments. Then, as I began to get the idea of her capability – it is surprising what can be transmitted just through the gripping of judo jackets – I threw her for yuko with *tomoe-nage* and then rolled her into *kame-shiho-gatame* for my second ippon.

Flanked by two of the biggest women in the 1986 World Championships. (left) Li, open category silver medallist and (right) Femgliah Gao, heavyweight gold medallist, both from the Republic of China and weighing in at 135 kilos each.

My third fight went much the same way. Zhangyun Li of China was clearly good in tachiwaza and newaza, and proved altogether a harder opponent. I couldn't quite connect with my standing techniques, though I went through the repertoire, and she proved skilful at avoiding my groundwork. But finally I caught her on the ground on all fours, and all those hours working on my rolls paid off yet again – I rolled her into *kame-shiho-gatame* for ippon, which put me in the final.

However, I had no illusions about Fumiko Ezaki, the 15-year-old Japanese girl who had reached the final. She was immensely strong, despite her age, having first appeared on the international scene as a 52 kilo player, and had obviously battled quite hard to get down to 48 kilos. She was also a judo fanatic, and quite a tough girl, with enormous cauliflower ears indicating that here was a dedicated groundwork fighter. She had thrown Fabienne Boffin and held her down with ease, so she had to be good.

I felt more relaxed, however, having reached the final. I joked about entering for the open weight category – until I stood next to Chiang Ling Li, the six-foot-two, 120 kilo Chinese player who eventually won a silver medal. And I went into the final confident and determined.

In fact, I had to draw on all my experience, because that junior high school student was very good indeed – certainly the best bantamweight Japan had ever produced. For two minutes I attacked her with everything I used, but all without producing a score, although I was well ahead on attacks. But I was only too aware that it only needed a koka for her to take away my title.

She had obviously studied my *tomoe-nage* in depth, and was killing it dead, and had even avoided being held down on a number of occasions. Suddenly, midway through the fight, I slipped past her guard and caught her with one of my fastest ever *tomoe-nages*. It looked as if she was going to sail over for ippon, but with remarkable presence of mind, she managed to twist out and only give away a yuko. I felt home and dry – so much so that I relaxed just three seconds from the end and allowed her to sneak in with her wrap-around *tani-otoshi* which scored a koka, although I thought I had twisted out of it sufficiently to prevent a score.

But a yuko is higher than a koka, and the match was won. I had retained my title, giving me three world titles in a row.

The thrill of winning my third title was magnified by the sense of relief after all the pressure. There was no way I was going to miss this particular official reception. In fact, I was going to make sure that everyone knew I was there. I had bought a slinky leather dress especially for the occasion, and after having had quite a few drinks, I decided I was going to shock everyone by walking into the reception smoking a cigar. A few foreigners were very surprised, and even came up for a closer look. It was not long before Ann, Diane and even Sharon were having a sly puff. I was only sorry that I had only bought a couple, one for me and one for Roy.

We celebrated late into the night – I danced with too many to remember. But I remember thinking that there couldn't have been a greater contrast between Ezaki and myself. I was experienced, dressed to kill and a little drunk, while she was clearly innocent, dressed in trousers, and practising

(a)

(a) and (b) Not the most flattering of photos, but this was the moment when I threw my Japanese opponent, Fumiko Ezaki, for yuko to clinch my third world title.

her *seoi-nage* turns while dancing. She was the perfect picture of a judo fanatic.

I had a bad night and not just because of the drink I had consumed. Almost without warning, the graze on my arm began to hurt considerably, and by the morning it had swollen up dramatically. It was tender and evidently full of pus. It was as if I had suppressed all those weeks of pre-competition tension with my powerful will to win, but it had eventually found an escape route – a little weakness in my system.

We were scheduled to catch a morning flight back to London, but even by then I was in terrible pain. I felt miserable on the plane and even cried, although there may have been an element of post-competition stress release. Rosie, the physiotherapist, looked after me, and took me to hospital as soon as we got to London. I was advised to go straight to the hospital in Hull, and Roy arranged for one of the Fairholme Judo Club members, Lee Rooke, to drive me up in my car. On arrival, I had to forgo the welcoming celebrations, going to the casualty ward instead where the arm was lanced. It needed five stitches, and was sore for a couple of weeks.

(b)

Three 1986 World Champions: (left to right) Diane Bell, under 61 kilos, Ann Hughes, under 56 kilos and myself, under 48 kilos.

Fourth Fukuoka International Championships

I did virtually no training, just tried to enjoy myself and bask a little in my achievement, although I had to remember that, come the middle of December, I had to be on the plane again, back to Japan for the fourth Fukuoka International Championships. This time, it was a much larger British contingent, with the world medallists, Dawn Netherwood and my old friend Ann Lucitt from Yorkshire and Humberside. Roy came with us too.

Everything was identical to the year before. In an extraordinary example of Japanese attention to detail, on arrival at the hotel, I was even given back a half-bottle of shampoo I had left there by mistake the year before.

Because I had done so little practice for the event, I had to watch my weight for a change. So, during the day, Ann, Sharon, Diane and I would don our sweat suits and go running in the hotel corridors for an hour – the only place sufficiently warm for us to raise a sweat. We were not very popular as we put a cassette player in the corridors and played our music quite loud to keep us going, until we were politely asked by the hotel staff to turn it down. While it is marvellous to stay in top hotels at competitions, it is not often easy to avoid conflict between the athlete's requirements and normal life.

I was really regarding the event more as a holiday than a serious competition, and I wasn't too worried whether I won or lost, even though I had won every one since it began. I felt I had done enough worrying about maintaining my reputation for one year, so I wasn't concerned about my lack of preparation, and just went out to do the best I could on the day. Boffin decided she too was here for a holiday, and couldn't even make the weight, which must have been a bit embarrassing after travelling thousands of miles at someone else's expense.

I found I faced three Japanese, and I went through the first two quite easily, meeting Ezaki in the final, as I expected. She had said in an interview beforehand how much she admired me, and that her ambition was to be like me, but of course to beat me, and I knew I had to find a little bit of the old magic to finish the year in style.

It turned out to be not only the last fight in the year, but the toughest, though perhaps that was partly because I was so unfit. We traded attack for attack. She had prepared even harder for this event, for it was very important to her to beat me on her home ground. And it was very close. She stopped all my major attacks, and adopted such an awkward stance that, if I had carried on with my normal attacking style, I would have lost on decision. I realised this about two-thirds through the fight, and changed my tactics accordingly, turning in for *tai-otoshi*, even though I only had control of one arm. The first attempt was so fast I nearly caught her with it too, but lacked the real control to turn her over.

The fight finished with no score. One corner judge gave the fight to Ezaki, and the other one to me. The referee from Hong Kong hesitated for a fraction, and then gave the fight to me. In fact, looking back at it over the

At home with Mum and Dad.

video, I think the decision was right, but I admitted in a post-match interview: 'She did give me problems, and I am going to have to reconsider the way I am going to fight her in future.' Nevertheless, I was pleased because most of the World Champions fighting that day lost.

On the plane home I was able to reflect on the extraordinary 12 months that had passed. It was my most disastrous from the point of view of injury, but the most successful from the point of view of competition. After all, I didn't lose once. In addition to the titles, I was also awarded a special prize from the *Yorkshire Post* Sports Council awards (it was against the rules to win it twice in a row) and the BJA presented me with a trophy as the sports personality of the year. My sideboard at home was getting even more heavily laden. And I also collected my 4th Dan, having amassed well over the required number of contest points.

Yet I was still only 23. I had won everything there was to win and I knew that the odds were against me continuing to take the top international medals year after year. But I still felt that I was capable of maintaining this peak level, and didn't feel that I was losing any of my strength, skill, speed, or – even more importantly – desire to compete and win. I was as keen as ever, and I was still enjoying my judo. I didn't seem to be jaded at all, which was perhaps partly a result of the constant variety in my life, one minute competing, the next minute in plaster, the next involved in a play, and the next competing again and getting plastered.

Above all, I still enjoyed training. This is the crux of the matter. If I still genuinely wanted to get out on the road running, or into the pool swimming, or on to the judo mat, I might as well continue. And in any case, there was one goal that I hadn't achieved.

The battle to get women's judo into the Los Angeles Olympics had been lost, but the International Olympic Committee could not deny the success of the sport. There was really no reason to refuse us entry to the Olympic movement. Sadly, they still managed to stall it, by saying that women could participate in the 1988 Olympics in Seoul, South Korea as a demonstration sport, but only be included in the main programme in the Barcelona Games scheduled for 1992.

Although I could see that it was unlikely, though not impossible, that I would still be around in 1992, I did want to participate in an Olympic Games, even as a demonstration sport. In the back of my mind there was also the possibility of the Commonwealth Games in 1990, when judo would be included on the main programme for the first time. It was for these reasons that I didn't really contemplate retirement in the Christmas of 1986, but I rested. Wisely, Roy Inman told all the World Champions that we were exempt from participating in the British Trials at the start of 1987 in order to justify our places on the British squad.

In fact, 1987 was going to be another hard year because it was to end in yet another World Championships. For although they normally take place every two years, the need to bring the men's event and the women's event together in order to fit in with the Olympic calendar meant that we had to join the men in Essen in 1987.

We could thus only enjoy our titles for one year – which was rather unlucky for Anne and Diane – before putting them on the line again. It was going to be another stressful year therefore, with the extra pressure because we knew that only those who won medals at the World Championships in Essen in 1987 were guaranteed a place in the demonstration event at the Olympics the following year. A slight slip on that German mat, and you were out of the Olympic running.

I can't say I started the year well. I made sure I enjoyed myself over the break, and, unusually for me, put on a stone and a half in weight. Not long before the event, I stepped on the scales and was horrified to see that I weighed nearly 56 kilos. I lost it in time for the French Open in Strasbourg, but didn't fight very well. Meeting Fabienne Boffin in my first fight, I was thrown for yuko with *uchimata*. I was bending over to pick her up with *te-guruma* as I had done in the 1986 Europeans, when I suddenly realised my leg was caught. I twisted out of most of the throw but conceded a yuko which I couldn't get back.

I came off angry with myself, and muttering: 'Well, I am not a robot, you know; you can't just bring me out and expect me to win all the time,' to which my training partner Sharon responded swiftly: 'Yes you are, get back in the cupboard until we have time to do the repairs.'

I wasn't too upset, but I was annoyed when I injured my knee shortly afterwards in a randori session. It meant I had to reschedule my programme and miss the German Open which I had counted on to help me build up for the Europeans. However, I managed to recover sufficiently to join the team in a training trip to Lanzarote organised, most imaginatively, by Roy. It was a week of hard conditioning, using the lavish sports facilities to their utmost. We ran, swam, did weights and circuits, and generally trained a lot harder, I must say, than most of the other international athletes making the most of the winter sun. In fact, some of the top British runners and field specialists couldn't quite work out what we did because we seemed to have such a high standard in most of the exercises we did. And there is no doubt that the British women's judo team are among the fittest women in the world of sport. I needed that week to raise my fitness level, and I worked hard, despite the lure of the sun and the enjoyable environment.

We did not do judo, but came back to London to a series of intensive judo sessions at Crystal Palace, in preparation for the European Championships in May in Paris. This was the first time that the men's event and the women's event would be held together, though this has been the standard format for athletics and swimming for years. It was very successful, even with the additional novelty of preliminaries on one day and finals on another, which meant we had to weigh in twice.

It was an enjoyable event for me. I didn't feel the pressure, which was a nice change, and won all my fights with ippon – though I nearly made a disastrous mistake. I armlocked Cinzia Amici of Italy in the first round, rolled and held down Barbara Eck of Austria in the second. This put me into the final against Anna Chodakowska from Poland. The Polish team had been improving consistently over the past few years, and I think I slightly underestimated Chodakowska, or perhaps I just had a momentary slip of concentration. As I went to take grip at the beginning of the contest, she suddenly swept my feet from under me. In fact, she nearly threw me for ippon. Fortunately, waza-ari was given. She had followed up fast, and I had to be a bit nifty to avoid being caught in a hold.

Eventually, we stood up. I must say that even at this point, I wasn't really concerned because I felt I could still win. I took hold of her – watching out for the footsweep this time, and threw her with *tomoe-nage* for yuko. I continued into groundwork, but we went off the mat. Then I caught her with another *tomoe-nage* for koka, and got into a controlling position on the ground before she could crawl to the edge of the mat. I went into my *sangaku-gatame* roll and within seconds had her firmly tied up in *kuzure-kame-shiho-gatame* for ippon. It was my fifth European title.

World Title in the Balance

An obligatory rest followed my European win, although not for long. The World Championships in Essen were scheduled for November, and I wanted a regular build-up.

In September I arrived with the women's team in Leonding in Austria for the Austrian Open and could only smile to myself when I found I had Boffin first fight. It went more easily than I had expected. I felt totally dominant from the start, threw her for yuko with *tomoe-nage* and was all over her for the remainder of the contest. Just as the bell sounded, I was turning her into a hold. With what appeared to be my greatest obstacle over, I relaxed a little – and paid the penalty. I faced Kirsten Emich, a tall West German girl, and as she turned in for *uchimata*, I attempted to counter with *te-guruma*. I had misjudged the length of her legs, and I was flung over on to my back for ippon. Whether or not it was a real ippon – I thought I had turned out of the full point – was academic. I was out of the contest.

It was the kind of warm-up I needed in one sense, although it did put me under more pressure than I really wanted for the British Open at Crystal Palace in October. I had trained hard for the event, and, frankly, it showed. By the time the day dawned, I looked drained and tired, evidently suffering from the pressures of defending my reputation on my home ground. I won through my pool without difficulty, but my fluency of movement was not there. I was like a professional going through the motions. Fortunately, my minimum standard was better than the maximum standard of most of my opponents. In the knockout section, I met a French opponent, Nadege Borelly, first, and held her down without much fuss. I was beginning to feel better already. Then came Kristina Pekkola of Sweden, and I threw her with *tomoe-nage* for ippon. At last I felt more my old self – and just in time, for Fabienne Boffin was next on the menu.

I had built her up so strongly as my main European rival that I couldn't believe how easily I dispatched her, throwing her for yuko, and then catching her on the ground in the middle of the mat, and, with my trusty old *sangaku* turn, rolling her into a hold.

Imagine how delighted I was, therefore, to find that I was in the final against none other than Kerstin Emich, the girl who had thrown me in Austria. Revenge, they say, is sweet . . . and it is. By the time the final came round, I felt completely relaxed and confident. More colour had come back into my cheeks, and I could hardly wait to get on the mat. She tried again to throw me with *uchimata*, but I had already prepared for that, and twice gained small scores with a pick-up counter that used my speed and manoeuvrability. But I was looking for the big one, an incontrovertible ippon that would settle the matter. It came from the unexpected quarter of a left shoulder throw, a technique I had been working on but which I had yet to use successfully in contest. Midway through the contest, I suddenly spun left and the tall Emich keeled over beautifully on to her back with a satisfying thud. There was no question about this score. It was a dictionary definition of ippon.

With this behind me, I felt more than ever that I was on the right track for my fourth consecutive world title. For the first time in a long while it seemed that I was injury-free in training and competition in the build-up to a big event. My left knee, which had given me some trouble, stood up very well to a couple of very hard weeks of squad training at Crystal Palace. I had no difficulty with my weight, yet I was eating well.

There was quite a bit of media interest before I flew off to Essen with the teams – for the first time, the men's and women's events were being held together, following the European pattern. The atmosphere in the women's team was good, and although the first of the four days brought no medals for Britain, days two and three more than compensated for this.

On the second day, Diane Bell was defending her title. And although she hadn't won a competition since the World Championships the previous year, she had obviously got peaking down to a fine art. She went straight through to the final and won with a clear throw. Meanwhile, Densign White, the middleweight, got a bronze in the men's event.

On the third day, I was delighted to see that Sharon Rendle, who had won a tough selection battle with Loretta Doyle to gain a place on the team, justified her place by winning the under 52 kilos title, and by beating two former world champions on the way. Ann Hughes, who was also defending her world title, lost in the semi-final, but came back to win a bronze, while lightweight Kerrith Brown also won a bronze.

Medal placing was particularly important for the women, because selection to the women's judo demonstration event at the Olympics depended partly on the medal winners, and partly on continental selection. But I felt confident as the fourth day dawned. I knew inside myself I had never been in better shape, physically or mentally, and I sensed that, all other things being equal, I was on course for a fourth title. The draw was acceptable, despite having Darlene Anaya, an awkward American for the first fight. The Chinese girl Zhangyou Liu, whom I had held down in the Maastricht World Championships looked my hardest opponent until the final, where I expected to meet Fumiko Ezaki.

Sadly, my luck was not equal to the event. I stepped on to the mat, bowed, and started to work. After three attacks, I scored a yuko for an *ouchi-gari*, and knew I was in good shape – the last time we had met, Anaya took me to a decision, although I wasn't in danger of losing that fight.

Then disaster struck. I turned in for a *tai-otoshi*, and my leg bent under me. But with my strong pull, I brought Anaya off-balance, and started to rise to complete the throw. As I did so, the American girl stumbled forward to stop herself being thrown, and her left foot came crashing down on my left leg

Disaster strikes in my fourth World Championships

with the sudden impetus of a karate kick. I collapsed and she dived for a strangle.

I waved to the referee to show that I was injured and matte was called. I felt there was something wrong with my leg, but I thought perhaps it was just a dislocation. I called over to Dr Kingsbury: 'It won't go back, what can I do to put it back?' He rushed on to the mat, but I wouldn't let him touch the leg, because according to the rules, any treatment means disqualification. He looked at it, and thought it was worse than just a dislocation, but I insisted. I tried to straighten it out, and then I tried to stand on it. I collapsed. Only then did I acknowledge to myself that my search for my fourth World Title was over for the moment – my leg was quite clearly broken, and broken badly.

I was put on a stretcher and taken off. Fortunately not ten minutes away from the Grugahalle, the stadium, was a hospital that specialised in breaks and an X-ray showed that I had two bad spiral fractures of the tibia and fibia. For three hours that afternoon I was on the operating table while two steel plates were inserted to keep the bones in position while they healed. It was not the way I had planned to spend the afternoon, or the evening – especially as the British team were celebrating a silver medal won by Elvis Gordon in the open category.

I came to in the morning. My father was with me – he had come to Essen without my mother who was herself not well again – but he was due to leave within a couple of hours. Roy Inman came to see me before he took the team back, and Dr Kingsbury stayed with me for two days. It was a miserable time. I couldn't help going over what might have been, and my leg was very sore indeed. I spent most of the time just crying. They were very good and kind in Germany, but I was glad to fly home although the journey – on a stretcher – was both painful and somewhat ostentatious.

I am writing this last section of my life so far in my hospital bed in London. There is no doubt in my mind that the story is incomplete as far as competition is concerned. I do not feel I have lost a title – incidentally, Liu won it in the end, beating Ezaki who, I am told, did not look her best.

I have been informed that I am due for another long period of convalescence, but I expect to be fully fit again by the summer of 1988 if not before. I don't know whether I will be allowed to compete in the demonstration event at the Olympics, although Roy Inman started a campaign for me the day after he returned to England. I feel my record alone should be enough to warrant special inclusion by the International Judo Federation.

I also know that when I get back to normal walking life, I will always have the memory of the accident emblazoned on my left leg – with a 12-inch long scar running the length of my lower leg (it needed 50 stitches). That is not an easy scar for a woman to bear – and I enjoy dressing up and looking good as much as any other woman.

But that is judo. I still don't regret the life I have had, despite the injuries and the tensions. I only know that when I am on the mat, and training hard, or competing, I feel more complete and fulfilled than at any other time. In that sense, I am lucky to have found judo.

MY TECHNIQUES

The 1986 Commonwealth Games in Edinburgh – I throw Porier of Canada for ippon with *tai-otoshi*.

8 Tachiwaza

Over the following pages I demonstrate the main throws I use in competition. Some people may be surprised that they appear to be only a few in comparison with the long list of judo throws included in most teaching books. Of course, all the leading international players have to specialise in just a few throws. If they go into a competition with too many to think about, they will get confused. If they go in to a competition with too few, they will not be able to meet all the likely obstacles placed in their path to the gold medal. So, the idea is to develop just the right number and then keep adding and subtracting to accommodate changing circumstances both in terms of individual capacity (one gets slower but hopefully wiser as one gets older) and external pressures.

These are the main throws I have used to win my world titles. They are not, however, the only throws I know or use. Roy Inman once said that he was confident that the top women in the British squad would be able to demonstrate at least 100 judo techniques, covering tachiwaza, newaza, combinations and variations. This shows that despite the selected repertoire we use in international events, they are the result of a much wider and highly intensive study. It may not be a good idea to take one of these techniques – say my *yoko-tomoe-nage* – and teach it to a beginner. It is important to have quite a few years doing the basic judo throws before seriously attempting to learn an advanced technique. Of course, it may come naturally by some chance. But I am convinced that I wouldn't have become a world champion earlier had I been taught the *yoko-tomoe-nage* at 14. I simply would not have been ready for it. Similarly, *te-guruma* would have been of little use at that early age because I simply wouldn't have had the strength to do it. So, the basic work is vital. Specialisation need not come before leaving the junior ranks, although players will automatically feel happiest using certain throws.

Now, after over a decade in judo, I find that I get most satisfaction from doing throws which are not the ones I normally practise. If I throw with *tomoe-nage,* I tend to look at it critically to see whether anything needs tightening up or improving. But if, in randori or competition, I suddenly throw with *osoto-gari* or *tsuri-komi-goshi,* or something I generally never do, I feel quite pleased. I feel that judo really is in my blood after all.

A word about my choice of throws: at first, I did throws that I enjoyed. This was true of *morote-seoi-nage* right at the beginning of my judo career, and of *yoko-tomoe-nage* after I learned it prior to my first World Championships. I then began to think of combining throws so that if one failed, I could go on to another. After that, I began to think of throws to deal with certain difficult styles, such as an extreme right-hander or an opponent with a very defensive posture. Basically, I was thinking about developing my own judo, of making a neat package which made the most of my strong points and which would give me a fairly wide range of attacks.

Only much later did I think of developing specific throws to deal with one or two particularly difficult opponents. This did not stop me planning how to fight women I met frequently at events. But the spotlight was on me and my techniques, not on how to get past opponent A or opponent B.

After all, I could spend months working on a particular technique to throw one player, only to find that she had moved up a weight category because she was too keen on ice-cream. In fact, I didn't think too much about opponents, and that is still true. Of course, I do the necessary homework on my main opposition. I watch them fight at the events and note their posture, their strong attacks, and what posture they need to attack. I consider my possible answers. Other than that, I do very little until I come to grips with them. I certainly don't spend hours watching videos of them. I just do my training, produce some basic plans, and get on and fight.

Yoko-tomoe-nage

(side sacrifice throw)

Introduction

I have probably had more success with *yoko-tomoe-nage* than with any other single throw. It seems to use my ability to twist and drop at high speed and to feel instinctively where I should throw. From one entry, the throw can go in many directions.

The basic technique was shown to me in time for the 1982 World Championships and it has surprised me that it still works at the very top level. I would have thought that people would have worked out how to stop it. Having said that, as the years passed, I was obliged to develop more combinations into the throw, for my opponents are not stupid. But I have caught everyone with it at least once, and often many times.

Opportunity

Unlike all my other throws, there is no 'best opportunity' for my *tomoe*. I know it more intimately than any other throw, but, perhaps curiously, I don't think calculatingly about it in competition. It just happens. I can see or feel an opportunity, for example a momentary defensive 'freeze' by my opponent, or I can set an opponent up for it. I can do it from a static position, or from general movement. But what normally happens is that in the process of moving around the mat, even with a defensive opponent, I suddenly feel the opportunity is there. It seems as if I move into a gear marked '*tomoe-nage*'.

Basic Movement

I visualise the whole movement not as a sacrifice technique, as taught in *nage-no-kata*, in which you fall on your back, but more as a backward roll. I aim to complete the circle so that if I throw or not, I invariably end up back on my feet again. This seems to have the added effect of making every attack a real one, whereas most people who use *tomoe-nage* have been penalised at some point or other for negative dropping. I never have, because even if it fails, I am up on my feet immediately

(a)

(a) to (h) *Tomoe-nage* straight over the top.

(b)

(c)

(d)

(e)

(f)

(g)

(h)

(a)

(b)

(a) to (g) *Tomoe-nage* over to my left, but with the main action coming from a driving right leg and a scissor action with my left leg.

(c)

(d)

(e)

(f)

(g)

from the sheer impetus of the attack. I never try to force it. If it fails, it fails.

Grips

I take a fairly standard grip, with my right hand on my opponent's left lapel and my left hand on the outside of my opponent's sleeve, above the elbow, holding the cloth firmly by the bicep. This gives me good control of my opponent's upper body which plays a crucial part in the throw itself.

Entry

1. My first movement is to step to my left with my left foot going past my opponent's right foot. This gives me more room to spin in for the throw, while at the same time encouraging my opponent to think that I am going for a right-handed throw. Having made the step, my left hand pulls high for a fraction of a second and my right elbow starts to come across my opponent's body. My opponent is now set up for the drop.
2. My right leg goes in and I drop. These two movements occur virtually simultaneously – you can see that even a camera with a motor drive advance has not been able to separate the two actions. The whole entry should be very fast – it should all feel as if one movement has been executed.

Ideally, my head should be placed by my opponent's advanced left foot. This is important, for the placing of the head dictates the precise placing of the foot. If the head is too far out, my foot will not be against my opponent at the right angle for the throw. I want my foot to be against my opponent's stomach, but parallel with the belt, not with the toes facing upwards.

Throw

1. My left arm now pulls strongly towards my head. My right arm pulls down so that my knee bends even more, like a spring being coiled up. At no point (so far) is my throwing leg straight. I want my opponent to be bending forward on to my leg, and if my throwing leg is straightened too early, it just pushes my opponent back on balance. My right elbow comes down to my side to bring my opponent even more on to the foot.
2. As my arms pull, my leg starts to spring up, taking my opponent well off her feet. To finish the throw, I flick the foot, extending the knee. It is this flourish that adds the final touch, and can make the difference between a low score and ippon. I want my opponent to spend as little time in the air as possible, otherwise she has an opportunity to twist out. This flick adds an extra boost of speed to her flight and she goes straight over the top.

Directions

The direction of the throw depends largely on how fast the spin is. The faster the spin, the more my opponent will go over my head. The slower the spin, the more she will go to my left.

If I haven't got my opponent coming forward very much at all, and she is pulling back, but my foot is in a good position, I can throw her to my right-hand side.

Otherwise, I can use my combination. I

(a)

(b)

(a) to (g) *Tomoe-nage* over to my right.

(c)

(d)

(e)

(f)

(g)

make a feint for *Kouchi-gari,* and as my opponent's right foot goes back to avoid it, I move smoothly into *tomoe-nage.*

Training

Yoko-tomoe-nage is a difficult throw to practise because you cannot do effective uchikomi without throwing every time. This is tiring for your partner, even with a crash-mat. So I do most of my uchikomi in randori. I make far more attempts at it than any other throw, looking for the bent posture that signals an opportunity, and always making sure I am doing it on the move.

Although I took to the movement quite naturally, it was nearly eight months before I began to throw opponents in competition with it. Like any throw, it takes time to develop.

Tip

Having got the basic idea from static uchikomi, always practise it on the move. Always visualise a smooth, unbroken, perfect circle described by your body dropping underneath and your opponent's body going clear over the top.

(a)

(b)

(a) to (f) My *kouchi-gari* into *tomoe-nage* combination.

(c)

(d)

(e)

(f)

Tai-otoshi

(body drop)

Introduction

Although *tomoe-nage* is my most successful technique, my favourite is *tai-otoshi,* though it is difficult to say why. A good *tai-otoshi* is very satisfying, perhaps because, in a good throw, tori finishes in a strong stance on both legs, while uke is placed quite firmly on her back. The ippon is indisputable. I had used it occasionally in my early senior days, but I really started to develop it after the work on *tomoe-nage* began – at least, in the grip work. Many international opponents continue to be caught with my *tai-otoshi* because they think they are blocking the *tomoe-nage. Tai-otoshi* is, of course, done in many ways, from many different grips; I use a number of variations myself. This is one of the most successful.

Opportunity

My opponent is defending strongly and not allowing me to stay squarely in front of her; most are worried about the *tomoe-nage,* or a *kouchi-gari* or *ouchi-gari.* At this point, I feel the opening for *tai-otoshi.*

Grips

My favoured grip is slightly unusual – it has been adapted through the years, and is a working compromise between what I need to make the throw work, and what I can generally get without provoking a grip-breaking manoeuvre. My left hand takes a low sleeve grip, or sometimes higher up, above the elbow. My right arm, which is the important arm for me, holds mid-label. I am looking for a strong rotational effect here, with my right arm lifting right the way through the technique (*see* (a)). *Tai-otoshi* is technically classed as a hand throw, and this is very much the way I feel it – my hands and arms do most of the work. And they start the movement, with a small pull with my left hand to bring my opponent on to her right leg. The pull happens simultaneously with my initial right foot step.

(a)

(b)

(c)

(d)

(e)

(f)

(g)

(h)

(a)

(b)

(a) to (g) *Kosoto-gari* into *tai-otoshi*.

(c)

(d)

(e)

(f)

(g)

Entry

The central element in the entry is speed. The basic idea is to step to the left side of my opponent with a strong half-circle swing of my left leg. In (b) this step is in mid-action, which looks like a strong and classical three-step action. But the whole movement is, in fact, fast rather than strong – it must feel like one blinding flash, though the hands must continue to work correctly. Very few photographers have actually caught this part of the throw in competition, because there is no indication that a throw is coming.

Throw

Classical *tai-otoshi* practitioners do not favour being so far to one side of the opponent, but I do. As can be seen in (d), at first my right leg is slightly bent, which ensures a deeper entry. The straightening action of the leg adds lift to the technique. It is important to remember to turn the head – this creates greater rotational impetus.

Training

Tai-otoshi has been successful for me because I worked on my suppleness. The more supple you are, the lower you can get to perform the throw, and the greater power you can generate in the end. I worked for a year on it to establish suppleness.

The surprise element is most important in my *tai-otoshi*, and that means speed. I therefore work on the grips and hand work separately, and then begin concentrating on the feet. I do many sets of ten uchikomi, setting my partner's feet with the right foot slightly forward, and working on the speed of entry.

Combination

Occasionally I add a *kosoto-gari* to the entry. Working from the extreme right-hand stance, I need a strong reaction to the *kosoto-gari* in order to get my opponent's weight on to her right foot – just as I would normally do with the initial pull. If my opponent does not step off my *kosoto-gari*, I will throw her with it backwards, rather than forwards with the *tai-otoshi*.

Ouchi-gake

(major outer hook)

Introduction

Many people feel that rear throws such as *kouchi, ouchi,* and *kosoto* only result in minor scores, but this is not necessarily true. It is possible to score ippon – and I have done so on a number of occasions with this technique.

Most of my big throws are to the front, and although this *gake* does not look particularly powerful, it has proved to be my most successful throw to the rear, partly because it appears deceptively weak, and partly because my opponents are generally defending strongly against my forward throws of *tomoe-nage* and *tai-otoshi*.

Opportunity

I want my opponent square on to me and defending strongly against a forward attack by pulling slightly backwards.

Grips

My grip is basically standard, although, as usual, I prefer quite a high sleeve grip, just above the elbow joint at the back of the bicep. I feel I can control the whole arm from here.

Stance

I stand with my right leg slightly advanced – fairly close to the leg I am about to attack.

Entry

I drive off my left leg, my right leg snaking around my opponent's left leg. My weight is really low, my right hand and right elbow pulling firmly down into the ground in order to pin my opponent's weight on to her left leg. My right leg hooks surprisingly low down – sometimes my weight is so low that I find I have dropped to my right knee. This can still be successful.

Throw

Once the entry has been achieved, the final push from the left-leg lunge enables me to drive hard against the opponent's chest, toppling her backwards. Impetus for the throw is created by hooking with the leg at the same time as driving with the right arm against the opponent's chest. With a good technique, the opponent feels as if she has been pole-axed. As can be seen, I continue my drive right down into the mat with my right hand, like the follow-through of a punch. Note the pointed toes of both feet – totally committed movement.

Training

I do sets of ten uchikomi, concentrating on the entry, getting the attacking leg into position. Sometimes I stand a mat apart from my partner so that I can practise reaching in from a long distance. Once again, suppleness plays a vital part.

For repetitive throwing, I use a crash-mat, which enables me to practise following through time and time again.

An improvised variation of *ouchi-gake* in the heat of contest – my right hand helps to tip Loly Veguillas of Spain backwards in the 1986 European Championships.

(a)

(b)

(a) to (g) *Ouchi-gake*.

(c)

(d)

(e)

(f)

(g)

Kouchi-gari into Ouchi-gake

(minor inner reap into major inner hook)

Introduction

I find that combinations into rear attacks are more successful than just direct attacks. Sometimes the combinations may be separated – I may attack with one technique, come out, and then attack with the real throw. At other times, as shown here, one technique follows directly into another, although this is generally a premeditated attack pattern, not a spontaneous movement.

Entry

I make a couple of *kouchi-gari* attacks, strong enough to make my opponent a little wary of them, but not totally committed. When she begins to react by stepping off the *kouchi*, I switch quickly into an *ouchi-gake* movement. Note that my attack is made from quite a way out – suppleness is again a key factor. But the real secret is smoothness and great speed: the *kouchi* movement can be at three-quarters speed, but the one–two change into *ouchi-gake* must be very fast indeed.

Training

A useful training method here is to let go of your opponent's upper body and, putting your hands behind your back, try to throw your opponent using your legs only.

(a)

(b)

(c)

(d)

(e)

(f)

(g)

Left Seoi-nage

(shoulder throw)

Introduction

This is another response to an opponent taking a right-handed high collar grip, but it plays an important part in my repertoire of throws for other reasons. It gives me an upright *seoi-nage* (whereas most *seoi-nages* done at top level are *drop seois*) and it is a throw to the left. However, it is a technique which needs total commitment, otherwise there is a risk of being taken backwards.

Opportunity

I generally use this against right-handed players using a high grip, though I can throw it from a variety of postures, using the advantage of total surprise – most of my throws are right-handed and a sudden change to the left can be very disconcerting.

Grips

To start with, I take a standard right-handed sleeve and lapel, but as the opponent reaches over for the high right-hand grip, my left hand slips underneath the right arm to take hold of the lapel. I find the double lapel grip strong, but I have to remember that I do not control the arms.

Stance

My initial position is quite important. I stand slightly to one side of my partner as the opening photo in the sequence shows. From here, I could duck under the arm and go behind for *te-guruma*, go in front for left *seoi-nage* or go over the arm for *yoko-wakere*. I want to see that my opponent's right foot is slightly forward – I must watch that because that is her working leg.

Entry

I bypass my opponent's front leg by moving in quite close on my right foot and spinning in, putting my left leg through the gap to a position fairly deep in between her legs. My right leg makes a small movement to catch up. Now my left hip can come strongly into the action.

Throw

I need a good, strong and flexible hip action to catch my opponent – I do not have control of the arms and the danger is that she will be able to spin out on an outstretched left hand unless I can lift her high enough and turn her well. However, I must not allow my hips to go too far through, because this weakens the posture and makes one susceptible to being pulled back. The lift is aided by the straightening of my knees and strong turn of my head and shoulders.

(a)

(b)

(c)

(d)

(e)

(f)

(g)

(a)

(a) to (c) My left *seoi-nage* in competition – in the 1986 European Championships.

(b)

(c)

Training

I do my uchikomi sets as a pattern. I take a double lapel grip. My partner takes a right-hand grip and starts to pull my head down, stepping forward in a realistically competitive manner. Then I do my uchikomi set of ten, as usual working on speed. Only then will I do five lifts, and finally go on to crash-mat work.

I concentrate not only on speed but also on firm control. I practise this as a standing technique, not a drop throw: only too often this kind of attack is seen as a failed drop – a flop.

Left Kosoto-gari into Left Seoi-nage

(minor inner reap into shoulder throw)

Introduction

As with my *tai-otoshi* on the other side, I use ashiwaza to create the opportunity for the big shoulder throw.

Throw

Having got my double lapel grip (there is not time to change grips later), I use the *kosoto-gari* to distract my opponent from the main attack. In fact, the *kosoto* opener makes my job slightly easier, for it forces my opponent to take her right foot back, a different stance from the one I attack in *seoi-nage* as a direct attack. But the attack against this different stance works equally well – in fact, I think it can make it even easier to spin through into the shoulder throw.

(a)

(b)

(c)

(d)

Te-guruma

(hand wheel)

Introduction

It was *te-guruma,* done as a direct attack rather than as a counter, that provided the answer to one particular problem – opponents who took a high right-handed grip. It is not a throw that is normally associated with women, because it does require a fair amount of lifting strength, as well as technique. However, this was where my consistent work at weight-lifting paid off, for it started to work for me fairly quickly, though I had already been using *te-guruma* as a counter for some time.

Opportunity

The signal for *te-guruma* comes from that high, strong right hand that is effectively preventing me from moving freely.

Grips

Once my opponent has settled with her high grip, I ensure that I have a mid-lapel grip with my right hand, but leave the left hand loose, or lightly hold the sleeve.

Entry

Letting go with my left hand, I push my opponent's elbow up slightly, creating a gap so I can slip my head underneath and behind my opponent. Pushing off the back foot, I move swiftly behind and place myself in a strong, lifting posture – bent legs but straight back. The greater the speed into position, the less power will be needed to lift, for you can catch the opponent falling slightly forward.

Throw

Clamping the opponent to me, I lift (with the legs, not the back) and then begin to turn my left wrist underneath the leg in order to turn my opponent on to her back. My right hand controls and guides more than anything else. I always follow the throw right through to the ground – if ippon is not called, there is often a good opportunity for groundwork.

(a)

(b)

(c)

(d)

(e)

(f)

(g)

(h)

Training

Once again, I feel speed is the most important factor, so I do many sets of ten uchikomi on the entry movement, practising raising the elbow and slipping past the controlling arm to get into position. I do not continue with the lift at this point – my weight-lifting routine is sufficient. But when I do practise the throwing, I generally use a crash-mat or lower my partner to the ground with consideration!

Te-guruma

(counter)

Introduction

I do not do very many counters – most of the time I am attacking myself, so there is no need. But I do use *te-guruma* as a counter quite a lot, particularly against *uchimata* specialists, who tend to use the high grip.

Entry

Balance and suppleness are important here. Feeling rather than seeing my opponent begin to attack with *uchimata*, I check my opponent's turn slightly with my right arm while at the same time begin to step over the reaping right leg. The timing must be right. Too slow, and I will get caught on the leg and thrown, which has happened to me on one or two occasions. Too fast, and I give the game away.

I must be sufficiently supple almost to do the splits standing on one leg, although often – as here – such an extreme stance is not necessary. But to have the confidence to rely on this counter needs supple hips and legs.

Throw

In the counter, I keep my head in front of the arm, not behind, and as a result, the direction of the lift is slightly different – there is more of a twist or a turn to my right to ensure enough height is gained.

(a)

(b)

(c)

(d)

(e)

(f)

(g)

Kouchi-gari with pick-up

(minor inner reap with pick-up)

Introduction

This came relatively late in my international contest career – I started to use it around 1984. I had been looking for a new way to open up a strong defence, particularly against my *tomoe-nage*. Opponents were not reacting to my *kouchi-gari* stepping action for fear of being caught on the *tomoe-nage* that would follow, yet they were able to ride the *kouchi-gari* itself. This was the answer.

Grips

I have a standard sleeve/lapel grip, from which I do my range of main throws.

Opportunity

I want my opponent's right leg to come forward, but hesitantly, so that she is clearly defending against a forward throw.

Entry

Standing fairly square to my opponent, I take a sharp step with my left foot to the side, but slightly backwards. This has the effect of bringing my opponent on to her right foot. I then lunge across with my right foot and just clip the back of my opponent's heel. This, coupled with firm control of my opponent's shoulders through my right hand, is generally enough to bring the foot off the ground.

Throw

If all this is done correctly, then a normal *kouchi-gari* follows. If my opponent's balance has not been broken completely, the assistance of the hand is all that is needed to take her on her back. As can be seen in (c), my opponent is losing her balance before my left hand has grabbed the ankle. But in (e), note the difference in the impetus once my hand has taken hold.

Training

I do regular uchikomi work on this. I need to practise covering quite a large distance quickly, and be low enough to pick up the foot. Speed and accuracy are essential.

(a)

(b)

(c)

(d)

(e)

Kosoto-gari-sticky-foot style

(minor inner reap sticky-foot style)

Introduction

This came fairly early on in my international career, and really because my opponents were not stepping off my attacking foot, being worried about the *tai-otoshi* that would follow. This shows how important it is to be able really to threaten with the first technique in a combination, even if the second technique is the main one.

Grips

Standard grip – sleeve, mid-lapel.

Entry

As can be seen from (a), I am standing slightly to one side, near the foot I am about to attack. I just reach out and scoop my opponent's foot off the ground – it is as simple as that. And just because it is so simple, it doesn't feel very threatening. Frequently, my opponents feel they can ride the attack quite comfortably – and they are still worried about withdrawing the foot because of a possible *tai-otoshi*.

Throw

I just keep on lifting, using my suppleness and balance, and controlling my opponent firmly with my right-hand collar grip, and high sleeve grip. At the stage shown in (d), my opponent still feels in control. At (e) she gets a sudden shock as she realises the danger. But it is too late. I can complete the throw by driving backwards.

Tip

It is tempting, on occasions, to try and force the throw and turn it into a kind of *yoko-gake* sacrifice throw. I never do this, for the chances are that on the way down the opponent can withdraw her foot and, at the last minute, counter with an ashiwaza herself. If you cannot control the balance from a standing position, come out and start again.

Training

I don't really do any special training for this other than the *kosoto-gari* into *tai-otoshi* uchikomi. But it can be useful now and again just to reap your partner's leg off the ground and practise driving backwards – in order to get the feel of the directional control of the hands and your own balance.

(a)

(b)

(c)

(d)

(e)

(f)

Yoko-wakare

(side separation)

Introduction

This is an example of a throw that I have practised and used in randori, but not in contest – perhaps because I have never been in a situation when my *te-guruma* or *seoi-nage* have failed against the high right-handed grip. However, most top players have throws in their repertoire which they do not use in contest, though they have a fair amount of success with it in randori. I may find myself using it in the future, or it may remain a randori technique for me. Nevertheless, *yoko-wakare* remains a slightly unusual though effective throw.

Opportunity

I started working on it as another answer to the high right-handed grip used by some of my strongest opponents. For *yoko-wakare*, however, I need my opponent to be bent over – too low to do my *seoi-nage* easily.

Grips

I pass my left hand over the top of my opponent's right arm and take firm hold of the lapel. My right hand hangs loose.

Stance

Ideally, I want my opponent to be slightly forward on the right foot. I can still do the throw if her feet are in line, but her weight must be substantially on her right foot. If it is on her left, she can step back slightly and block against the drop, smothering the technique entirely and leaving the thrower in a very dangerous position on the ground.

Entry

Making sure that my opponent has not managed to straighten up, I grasp her extended arm in *ippon-seoi-nage* style (a very strong grip is crucial) and at the same time throw myself completely into the mid-air spin. I must ensure that I hit the ground on my side, not on my back.

Throw

The throw feels similar to a *makikomi* – you are winding yourself inside your opponent's arm and rolling her over. This doesn't sound very incisive, but the results can be very spectacular indeed.

Combination

If, having taken the initial over-arm collar grip with the left hand, your opponent manages to stand upright, the opportunity arises for the more conventional right-handed *ippon-seoi-nage* – standing or drop form.

Training

I don't do any special training for this at all. I think that most people who do this have a feeling for the throw in their mind's eye, and just throw themselves into it when the moment arises.

(a)

(b)

(c)

(d)

9 Newaza

Tate-shiho-gatame (four quarters hold)

It was with a variation of this, my favourite hold, that I won my second world title and I have won many contests with it over the years. It is not an easy hold, because many people find that they are easily rolled over. But my suppleness allows me to get the maximum spread of the legs as the photo shows. This, combined with a very strong upper body grip, makes it a position of extreme discomfort for my opponent. In short, once they are caught in it, they do not want to struggle very much. I feel that every corner of my body is working. Not only are my arms working strongly to hold firmly, though without being rigid, but my legs are actively working on a spreading effect. There are no loose edges.

This came from regular groundwork practice not only with other women, but also with teenage boys at club level. Boys in their mid-teens who have reached blue and brown belt level provide just the right

Tate-shiho-gatame – my favourite hold.

opposition, because they are strong and competent without having a man's strength or a man's ego. It was extremely useful for me as I methodically developed my groundwork after winning my first world title to get these boys into holds and then control them for 30 seconds or more. Gradually I began to be able to compete realistically with older and stronger men. But these early practices allowed me to develop my newaza. They showed me where my technique was failing or the control was good – which is more difficult when working against a grown man's muscular defences.

Perhaps if I had continued to work mainly with men – there being relatively few high grade women in dojos – I would have undoubtedly developed a strong defence, but possibly not very creative or effective attack patterns. I do other holds, including *kame-shiho-gatame* and *yoko-shiho-gatame*, and have scored frequently with armlocks and even strangles. But in the end I feel happiest with osaekomi-waza, where I know I am in control.

It has been said that you have to have natural talent to be a good throwing technician in judo, but that you can *learn* to be fearsome in newaza. I tend to agree with this. I set out to improve my groundwork over a period of time, step by step, and those hours of uchikomi have certainly paid off. So, while enjoying your standing work, don't neglect your groundwork. To the untutored eye, there is little to compete with a spectacular throw that produces ippon. But the educated judoka will always deeply appreciate the deft, quiet power demonstrated by a newaza technician who makes a muscular, defensive opponent look as vulnerable as a babe in arms.

Sanguku-jime into Kame-shiho-gatame

(triangular strangle into upper four quarters hold)

Introduction

This is my most successful move in newaza. I started working on it seriously after winning my first world title, and I was able to depend on it for competition after competition, particularly from my second world title onwards. I have demonstrated it in one direction, but I can do it equally well the other way – I didn't want to find myself prevented from smooth transition from tachiwaza into newaza by the constraints of a red line.

I like this move because it offers a combination of good control at every stage in the technique, while allowing sufficient variation to take account of different circumstances. Therefore, I can attempt the strangle, and if that doesn't work, go on to the hold, or even an armlock. I generally prefer to slip into *kame-shiho-gatame*, however, where I feel secure and totally in command.

(a)

(a) My opponent is in the standard defensive position, guarding her arms and neck. I start working from behind my opponent (this enables me to choose which side I attack) but always ensuring that my weight is on her, controlling her. If my opponent blocks with the left arm and there is room for the manoeuvre, I go for the right arm (it sounds simple, but it is effective). In many ways, the hardest part of the whole technique is the start – getting hold of the wrist.

(b)

(b) to (e) Here, the right arm has come under the armpit, grasped the wrist, and pulled the arm in tight. Still controlling my opponent with my weight, I move round to begin the roll.

(c)

(f) and (g) This is the next major stage. I

need to do two things, more or less at the same time. I need to consolidate my hold on the arm – my left hand now comes into play, taking hold as well – in addition to moving my right leg over my head. I need to insert my foot between my opponent's left arm and left leg – under the left armpit is an ideal which is not always possible. This is the stage where it is most likely the opponent will be able to escape if the whole action is not smooth and yet tight.

(h) and (i) Drawing my opponent over with the hands – the feeling is similar to using a lever – I fall to my right side. The action of the legs must be firm but not rigid. A certain amount of adjustment is needed during that falling action in order to bring the opponent round into the correct position. Rigid clamping on the turn stops the fluency of the technique.

It may be necessary to straighten out the opponent by releasing the legs slightly. I can pull on my opponent's left arm to help turn her a little but often the problem is that my right leg gets caught slightly underneath my opponent's back. It just needs to be brought out so that my opponent's head is neatly pillowed on the inner thigh. If the position is perfect, the strangle, *sangaku-jime*, is now possible. If it doesn't come on, try pushing away the arm trapped in between the legs – this puts extra pressure on the neck. Failing that, it is possible to take the wrist and attempt an armlock, but most experienced opponents will grab cloth to prevent this. It may be necessary, therefore, to go into the next stage of the movement.

(j) and (k) This is the tie-up action. With my right hand still controlling the wrist of my opponent, I stretch out my left hand to pick up the bottom of uke's jacket and feed it into my right hand. This helps to immobilise my opponent and ensures a very secure hold. It is worth spending time on

(d)

(e)

(f)

(g)

(h)

(i)

(j)

(k)

(l)

(m)

(n)

this tie-up so that it is extremely tight. It is virtually impossible to escape from a hold where this is properly done – at least, no one has ever escaped from me once I have tied them up in this way.

(l) to (n) It is now relatively easy to sit up into *kame-shiho-gatame*. Your opponent may struggle for a little while, and you may have to wait a little for the right moment, but at some point, the opponent will stop the fruitless struggle for a second. This is the time to move into the hold. Reaching over with my left hand to grasp the belt or side of my opponent, I swing my left leg around, bringing my opponent's left arm with it. Practice can make this movement very smooth, even with a very resistant opponent. Last of all, I settle back into a comfortable *kame-shiho-gatame*.

(a)

(a) to (d) Detail of the tie-up in *sangaku-jime* into *kame-shiho-gatame*.

(b)

(c)

(d)

Arm Roll Combination

Introduction

Of course, no techniques in judo are unstoppable. My opponents learned to hinder and, on rare occasions, actually stop the *sangaku* roll by putting out their left leg to 'prop' against the roll itself. Most of the time, I can overcome it, but I also have the option of using their force to my advantage.

(a) and (b) I appear to be moving in for the normal *sangaku* roll, but I notice that my opponent has propped well with her left leg.

(a)

(b)

(c)

(d)

(e)

(c) to (e) I push off fast from my right leg, gaining a strong impetus and swing into the left-straddle position.

(f) to (h) The sudden switch has utilised all the pushing power of my opponent, and the actual roll, aided by my left hand, is fairly easy.

(f)

(g)

(h)

(i)

(j)

(k)

(i) This is the danger point. If the opponent is flexible and gymnastic, it is possible for her to turn towards me and move into a hold. I should be able to stop it by fast movement and my right arm, but it is a threat I must be aware of.

(j) and (k) Once I have reached this stage, it is relatively easy to move into *kame-shiho-gatame*.

Training

I do regular uchikomi training on both *sangaku-jime* and this arm roll – they have to feel second nature. I vary the uchikomi, sometimes working on control and accuracy, and sometimes on speed. I also work to get the wrist – if I can't get the wrist, I can't start the movement. So I do many sets of going for the left but taking the right, and vice versa.

Juji-gatame Roll

(armlock)

Introduction

This is a popular move, used with great success by Neil Adams, but I started to use it fairly late in my career, and mainly as a follow-on combination to my *sangaku* roll.

(a) With my opponent on all fours, I start at the opposite side to the arm I am going for. I feed my left arm through the opponent's right arm from the front, though often it is necessary to create a gap myself – once again, the start of the movement is the hardest part. Once this has been done, I know that the move is on, and I bring my right leg over my opponent's back.

(b) I place my left leg on the back of my opponent's head, making sure that my weight is on the back the whole time in order not to lose control. At this point, I pull in tightly with my left arm, using the right arm as an extra aid, so that I can work an efficient lever effect in the forthcoming roll.

I start the roll by pushing on the back of the head with the shin and pulling strongly on the arm. This push/pull effect helps to stretch out the opponent to begin the roll.

(a)

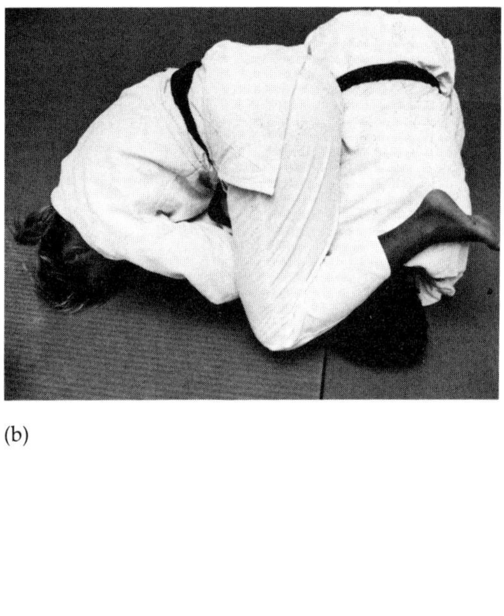

(b)

(c)

(c) I turn to face the direction of my opponent's feet. It is the leverage effect of the arms that forces my opponent to go with the roll, although the movement is aided by the use of the legs.

(d) and (e) I now find myself in classic *juji-gatame* position, and work on straightening out the arm in order to get the submission.

(d)

(e)

Juji-gatame into Tate-shiho-gatame

(armlock into four quarters hold)

Introduction

Some opponents are extremely strong in the upper body and can resist the armlock by clasping their own arms. I generally don't fight this too much, because I find it much easier just to bypass the resistance by moving into a hold.

(a) and (b) From the stalemate *juji-gatame* position, I let go with my left hand (always ready, however, to snap on *juji-gatame* with my right hand if the opponent tries to escape).

(c) and (d) Pushing my right hand through further to give more space to the forthcoming turn, I prop myself on my left hand and start to twist. However, I keep myself as low as possible, so that my opponent does not feel a sudden release of controlling pressure. I take my right foot slightly back, and move into the splits position – obviously, this technique is only possible for supple people.

(e) and (f) Ensuring continuing control with my right arm – notice how I lean forward to gain extra contact – I pass my left leg through. This movement must be smooth and fast, because my opponent will sense a chance to escape and will start struggling.

(g) and (h) I then move into *tate-shiho-gatame*, concentrating on good chest control and, last of all, tightening the legs.

Training

Uchikomi is vital for both these movements. It is worth while learning to do them on the right and left. I get my partner to offer increasing resistance, so that by the end I am working against quite an unwilling partner.

(a)

(b)

(c)

(d)

(e)

(f)

(g)

(h)

Sideways Roll into Kame-shiho-gatame

(upper four quarters)

Introduction

I use this turnover quite often in competition and randori. It is simple but effective – two qualities which often go side by side in judo – but it does require confidence in newaza because in the course of the technique, it is necessary to roll on to your back which is a risk situation.

(a) The opponent is defending on all fours and I am attacking from the left side. As always in these situations, I keep my weight well down on my opponent's back to control her. Gradually, I work my right arm through a gap created underneath my opponent's left armpit, and force it through sufficiently to grip my own lapel. This is a little uncomfortable for me, but much more so for my opponent.

(b) My left arm now passes by the head and takes hold of the collar on the opposite side.

(c) As can be seen, I then stop just past the head – but this is a feint only. I am trying to convince my opponent I am taking her in that direction, so that she begins to brace against it, pushing towards her left.

(d) This is the crucial moment. I bring the leg back sharply and spin on to my back as fast and as powerfully as possible. With both legs out in front, I can produce quite a good spinning impetus which I need to take me well over to my left side.

(e) As I go, I tuck my head under the armpit allowing me to emerge . . .

(f) . . . on the other side. My opponent is drawn inexorably on to her back.

(g) And I can settle comfortably into *kame-shiho-gatame.*

Tip

When completing the roll, I think about controlling the upper body. Sometimes I find that the momentum of the roll is too fast, resulting in the opponent going too far through and then finding herself able to sit up. If I am in control of the upper body, I can bring them back for the hold down.

Training

Speed is essential here, because it provides the surprise element. A sloppy turn means that there is a very real danger of getting caught half-way through the technique – with the opponent on top.

(a)

(b)

(c)

(d)

(e)

(f)

(g)

Defence in Groundwork

Introduction

My attitude to newaza is that attack is the best form of defence. I do not like working off my back and do my utmost not to be caught on my back in competition. Equally, I don't like defending from all fours. In fact, it is very rare to see me defending in competition because I go to a lot of trouble to make sure that I am always in the dominant position, attacking positively. However, there are times when defence is the better part of valour, and all judo players must be able to defend as well as attack. What follows may appear to be a little negative because it is a stalemate situation, but sometimes momentary tactical stalemates can result in victory in the end.

(a) I have caught my opponent between my legs. Her job is to get past my legs, and the way I stop that is by controlling the upper body first. Then I wrap my feet around her.

(b) Often I can only catch one foot, but if I can control her upper body well, I am not in too dangerous a position. I take my left leg over my opponent's right leg just behind the back of the knee.

(c) The next step seems more complicated than it actually is. I take my right leg over my own left leg, and then hook my opponent's foot. By straightening my leg, I am able to control my opponent's foot and leg completely. It is now virtually impossible for her to get it out. It is distinctly uncomfortable for my opponent, and will eventually end with the referee calling matte. However, this is something I use rarely in randori against heavyweights. It is not often I am caught defending on my back in competition.

(a)

(b)

(c)

Training

I work with my partner to make sure that this move is second nature. I know that if I ever need it in a contest, it will be only at a time of great pressure, so I must be able to do it without thinking too much. I repeat the move on both sides five or ten times. Then I give my partner 30 seconds to get her leg out in any way she can.

Obi-tori-gaeshi

(belt grab turn)

Introduction

This is a technique that I practise and occasionally use in randori but have yet to use in contest. This is principally because I generally work from my opponent's back and I try to avoid going on my back in groundwork. This technique centres on a backward roll and if it goes wrong, I could end up in a very disadvantageous position. Nevertheless, I practise it because one day I may need to use it to get me out of trouble – and if that happens just once, I feel all the work will have been worth while.

(a)

(a) and (b) Most of my newaza attacks are from the back of my opponent, but here I am at the front. I am demonstrating it from the best position, when I am clearly dominant. But I can start *obi-tori-gaeshi* from a sitting position, so long as I make sure to sit upright, keeping my back off the ground until the move has begun. It is very dangerous to try the move when lying flat on your back, because you cannot effectively control your opponent.

(b)

(c)

(c) A good grip is crucial to the control throughout the technique. I pass my left hand under my opponent's arm, grasp the belt, and take my right hand over the back also to hold the belt. I keep my right arm more or less on the right side of my opponent's head.

(d) and (e) Now the main movement begins. I come up on my feet and, crouching on my left leg, slip my right foot in between my opponent's legs, keeping it fairly bent. In the same movement, I pull myself close in to my opponent, forming the top half of a circle.

(d)

(e)

(f) to (h) Pulling hard, mainly with the right arm, I roll backwards, flipping my opponent over my right shoulder with my right leg. My right elbow maintains continuous pressure on the shoulder blades to keep my opponent bent over and prevent her from spinning out in mid-air, which is the main way to escape from the move.

(f)

(g)

(h)

(i) and (j) The impetus of the whole movement should be sufficiently confident to take me over into *tate-shiho-gatame*, as it has done here. It is necessary to be aware of the legs, particularly in the final part of the roll, for it is at this point that the opponent will attempt to catch one of them to prevent the hold going on. This awareness comes with practice.

(i)

Training

I do uchikomi in sets of five or ten to build up speed and to learn to use my legs to control my opponent on the turn. Many girls and women may think that they are not strong enough to do this kind of technique, but it is not a question of strength. It is more the momentum of the roll, and the ability to flick the opponent over with the leg.

I do not attempt to use *obi-tori-gaeshi* until I feel I am in complete control – and that means having the ability and confidence to control an opponent between the legs. Attacking from this position is not easy. It is necessary to learn to control from this position and feel safe first, and only then learn to attack.

(j)

10 Supplementary Training

Fitness

Fitness is as important to me as judo itself. Not only do I enjoy the feeling of being fit, but I actually enjoy the work involved in getting fit. I am not happy when a day goes past without running or swimming or working out in one way or another. In that sense, I haven't changed since I was a child.

My attitude towards fitness has changed over the years, however. I have learned to take a more scientific view in order to ensure that I am correctly prepared for competition. This means cutting down on some things I like – such as extended runs – and increasing specific weight training; and learning about pulse-rates, aerobic and anaerobic work, glycogen, and all the other bits of basic body chemistry that an athlete needs to know. For getting fit is as much a skill as judo itself. The wrong preparation training can leave you with great endurance but no explosive power; pumped up muscles that look impressive but lack real use; or marvellous flexibility but no strength at maximum extension.

I have seen girls coming into the junior squad thinking that they are fit because they go for a run now and again, and being absolutely horrified by the work-load they encounter – in fact, I was one of those once.

What can be surprising from looking at my schedule is the amount of fitness work I do in relation to judo, both randori and specific skills training. There are a number of factors to be taken into consideration here.

It did not surprise me to discover that in the Eastern Bloc countries the top judo competitors spend as much as 70 per cent of their time in supplementary training of one kind or another. Judo at the top level places such severe physical demands upon the individual that only with peak fitness can the international competitor hope to make her techniques work against experienced opposition. Perhaps pure skill can produce one or two superb wins in the early rounds, but it is no longer possible for a competitor, man or woman, to last through six or more rounds to a final without outstanding fitness. This is the harsh reality of modern judo.

The traditional response to this is that the best way to get fit for judo is to do judo. But the injury rate when techniques are being attempted with full commitment is bound to be high, and it is simply more efficient to separate fitness training from judo. Roy Inman dislikes squad members coming on to a randori wearing sweat gear beneath their judogi. His argument is that extra clothes means that they will struggle to last a full session – and on the judo mat they are supposed to be developing judo skills, not losing weight or just 'having a good sweat'.

The other aspect to bear in mind when looking at my supplementary fitness work in relation to my judo skills work is that I have been doing judo for well over ten years – for the past seven years at international level. I have done an immense amount of judo. My basic range of skills has been formed for a long time. I no longer add to the basic range of movements, but make small improvements here and there. Only occasionally do I add something totally new, and even then it will probably be a variation of something I do already.

So my supplementary training routines must be taken in this context, and not followed by young players who need, first and foremost, to get a lot of judo behind them. Having said that, I firmly believe that up to the age of 16 or so the most important thing is to do lots of sports. The greater the variety, the better – within reason.

The primary commitment may be to judo, but running, gymnastics, swimming, football – even racket games like tennis and squash – all offer something to aid judo.

Training Disciplines

Running

I have always loved running. Long distances, short distances, hill work, running on grass, roads, tracks, cross country – I enjoyed it all. Running cleans out the body, gets the cardio-vascular system going, and is mentally invigorating. It is important for basic stamina work, though on a more specific level, different kinds of run work in different ways.

Sometimes I run for just one and a half miles, but wearing full sweat gear. I do this when I am nearing a competition and have to watch my weight a little. As I get older, I have to be a little more careful with my weight, but I would rather eat and run than starve and sit.

When I was young I felt that it was good to do long runs, and I would set off for eight or nine miles along the roads, and even do a judo session afterwards. At one point I was so keen that I used to do it with weights strapped to my ankles. It was fun at the time, but probably was the basic cause of my knee injuries, and it was unnecessary.

Running is important for stamina, but to keep in shape, three or four miles is probably enough. That is my basic distance now and I tend to do it reasonably fast – somewhere between 17 and 23 minutes. I try now to run on grass where possible in order to relieve the pressure on my knees, the only problem being that it generally means I have to go round a small circuit which does get a bit boring. But at least it stops me getting lost. My general principle when I run in a strange town is to keep on turning right, but there have been times when I have been out for an hour or more looking for the way back to my hotel. I now tend to run in hotel corridors.

I also tend to do shuttles daily – six sets of six lengths of the dojo. I do them with a partner so that one of us is always resting.

Skipping

I started this in 1982. It is basically a stamina exercise, although it is also a good way to lose weight. I took to it quite easily, of course, not only because of childhood games, but also because it enabled me to indulge in my enjoyment of counting developed during tap the ball competitions. I tend to skip 2,500 times which takes me about 20 minutes.

Exercise Bike

I have had an exercise bike in my house in Hull for some years. After winning my third title, I treated myself to a new one with computer read-out and other extras. I use it to work the legs specifically. I do about 25 miles on it – at five minutes a mile speed – and at a fairly low tension.

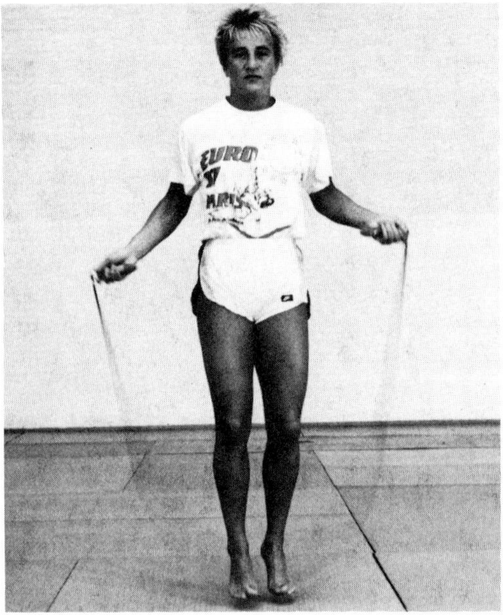

Skipping – a good stamina exercise

Cycling

I cycle fundamentally for pleasure – I like the sheer physical sensation of travelling on a bike. I will cycle down to my physio and back and do up to 20 miles, really for sheer enjoyment.

Swimming

I started swimming in 1983. It is basically cardio-vascular work, making sure that the breathing is deep and rhythmical. I tend to do between 50 and 100 lengths of a 25-metre pool, mainly front crawl with some breast-stroke. I will do them in one set of 50 followed by five sets of ten, with a short break in between, or one set of 50 if I am doing 50 lengths. The only way to do distances like that is to get the breathing absolutely correct. I noticed the difference in my judo quite early on and now I never pant on the judo mat. I may get tired, but never out of breath in a randori.

Because the main work in swimming is done by the arms, it has the added effect of keeping the shoulders loose. The swimming motion is very therapeutic and generally tones and shapes the body in a pleasant and safe manner.

Stretching

I was not very flexible as a youngster and had to spend quite a few months at 17 or so improving my suppleness. I went to a few karate lessons to see how they did it, and then worked hard in my room on my own for at least 45 minutes a day. The suppleness came.

Now I just have to maintain suppleness, which is not so hard. Every time I warm up, I go through a suppling routine, working on the major joints of the body. Now and again I may have an extra-long session, particularly if I feel a little tight in the muscles through some hard judo or weight training sessions.

Trampolining

This is very useful for developing spatial awareness – knowing where you are in the air. I haven't had to spin out of throws very often, but the trampolining I have done has given me that basic awareness when I am upside-down. It is also surprisingly demanding on both strength and suppleness. This is only a very occasional practice.

Circuits

This is an all-body training routine. I vary it considerably, but each time I make sure I work each of the major muscle groups, and my cardio-vascular system. I will decide my routine for the day, and then do three full circuits.

Sit-ups 30
Press-ups 30
Squat thrusts 30
Squat jumps 30
Jack-knives 30
Sprint starts 30
Step-ups (on bench) 30
Sprints across the crash-mats (like running in a marsh) 5 lengths of the dojo
Light weights curls and upright rowing

On the last circuit, depending on how I feel, I may increase the numbers to 50. As a variation, sometimes I may do 30 seconds of each exercise rather than 30 repetitions.

Weight Training

I have found weight training a very interesting part of my fitness work. Many women do not enjoy weights, and shirk them where possible. But I know the difference they have made to my judo. The myth remains that they slow you down and load you with muscle bulk which is not good for judo. But it is all a question of what kind of weight training you do.

(a)

(b)

(c)

I started when I was 16 or so, at the dojo after a run and a swim. At first, it wasn't a proper practice – I would just lift a few weights. But between 1983 and 1984 I started a proper weights circuit, and did a weight training coaching course in Hull, which taught me a lot.

At first, I did feel quite stiff, but gradually I learned what I needed and what suited me best. I could always go back to work on my speed at a later stage – when I had increased my strength.

With a proper weights programme, the strength factor increases quite rapidly. It also goes quite quickly, although it is possible to maintain much of the increase with a fairly light practice.

I now plan my weights programme very carefully, taking into account my competition schedule. I generally work towards a very big event like a World or European Championships. The basic idea is to build a base of strength well in advance of the event, maintain it, and then taper off as the competition nears. My sharpness on the mat suffers but I deal with this at the next stage when I work on judo technique and then, finally, sharpen up everything by concentrating on speed.

Programme

Four months before the event I start on light weights and plan to reach my maximum over a period of eight weeks. When I start, the programme will take me about one hour and ten minutes. By the end of the eight weeks, I will be spending up to two hours and fifteen minutes on the programme.

I do my weights in two ways. Either upper body on one day and legs on another. Or I do the whole programme every other day – Monday, Wednesday, Friday, Sunday, then Tuesday, Thursday and Saturday.

For the upper body:

1. Clean and press 5 times, 8 repetitions; 10kg plus bar (minimum) rising to 30kg (maximum).
2. Curls 5 times, 8 repetitions; 10kg plus bar rising to 30kg.
3. Upright rowing 5 times, 8 repetitions; 10kg plus bar rising to 30kg.
4. Press behind neck 5 times, 8 repetitions; 10kg plus bar rising to 25kg.
5. Reverse curls 5 times, 8 repetitions; 10kg plus bar rising to 30kg.
6. Bent arm pullover 5 times, 8 repetitions; 10kg plus bar rising to 20kg.
7. Bench press 5 times, 8 repetitions; 15kg plus bar rising to 35kg.

For the lower body:

1. Squats 5 times, 8 repetitions; 15kg plus bar rising to 35kg.
2. Calf raises 5 times, 8 repetitions; 15kg plus bar rising to 40kg.
3. Reverse leg curl 5 times, 8 repetitions; 10kg plus bar (no increase).
4. Leg curl 5 times, 8 repetitions; 20kg plus bar rising to 40kg.
5. Sit-ups on incline 5 times, 10 repetitions on third level ladder with 2.3kg.

Finish with a warm down.

This is my basic weights programme. Some competitors do specific weights for judo, but I just use weights to build strength, and it seems to work for me. Sometimes I vary it slightly. When the weights get very heavy, I may drop down to five sets of five – it depends how I feel.

Once I have attained my maximum over eight weeks, I stay at maximum for two weeks, doing the weights three times a week. This consolidates the strength. However, by this time I will already be starting a busy fitness and judo routine too, so it can be quite a tiring period.

With the competition a little over two months away, I cut right back to just one long weights session a week. This is sufficient to keep most of the weights gains I have achieved over those gruelling eight weeks. I never miss a weights session, because building the base is so hard that it can be unpleasant coming back. So, every seven days, I do my weights routine.

I do most of the basic weights work on my own in my room at home. By the time I get to my maintenance programme, I am generally in London. It is necessary to be quite cautious when working weights on your own. Once, when doing a bench press, I had done too much and couldn't lift it off my chest. I had to yell for my mother to come up, but she couldn't really help because she couldn't lift the bar either. We managed to roll it down my body in the end. This is the kind of accident that can happen.

Daily Routines

These vary somewhat depending on where I am and what facilities I have. But what follows are typical examples of my days.

Four Months before the Event

From 9 a.m.: warm-up; 3-mile run; exercise bike, 15 minutes; 100 sit-ups; exercise bike, 15 minutes; 100 sit-ups; 2,000 skips; 5 sets of 20 press-ups; check weight – I reckon to lose about five pounds.

Finish between 10.30 a.m. and 10.45 a.m., perhaps with a short sauna, followed by a pint of Diet Coke or fruit juice. At 11.30 a.m. I have a breakfast of cornflakes, toast and tea followed by rest.

At 1.30 p.m. or 3 p.m. I go swimming or do weights for one and a half hours. My main meal of the day is at 4 p.m. or 5 p.m. I do better when I am at home – in London I have to make an effort to eat good food. I must admit, I consume quite a lot of what is generally termed junk food.

In the evening, I will sometimes go to judo, but at this point it is strictly for enjoyment. I will go on with the kids, do some uchikomi, perhaps some randori, but at this stage in the build-up, fitness is the key, not judo.

Two Months before the Event

From 9 a.m.: warm-up; 3-mile run; uchikomi – sets of 10, 250 to 300 in all; 30 minutes of uchikomi on the move; 30 minutes of crash-mat work, covering a range of attack and counter routines, perhaps ending with newaza uchikomi; 30 minutes of fitness, skipping, exercise bike, sit-ups, etc.; warm down and/or sauna.

After lunch I either swim 50 or 100 lengths or do a circuit. Then I rest to recuperate for the evening. In the evening I do judo, on three or four evenings a week, sometimes travelling around the clubs in order to get different randori partners. How much randori I do depends on what other training sessions are arranged – such as the intensive weekend squad sessions at Crystal Palace. If I am training all weekend, I will do less during the week, though before a big event I will train between three and five times each week.

Two Weeks before the Event

From 9 a.m. wearing full sweat gear: warm-up; one and a half mile run; shorter fitness programme (I should now be as fit as I can be) involving 15–30 minutes on the exercise cycle and 15 minutes skipping; uchikomi, tachiwaza; uchikomi on the move; shuttle runs; sit-ups; warm down; sauna.

My afternoon training depends on my weight – I may still swim. In the evening I do intensive randori.

One Week before the Event

I do virtually nothing, just one or two runs a day, and only a little uchikomi, if anything at all. I like almost a full clear week before the big day. I am primarily concerned with keeping my weight in check and keeping my system alert with a good sweat every day.

11 The Competition World

Competitive Attitude

When I was young I went in to any and every competition I could. To say that I felt extremely competitive is an understatement. Even in randori, the feeling was the same. Many people felt that it didn't matter so much whether they won or lost, but I didn't think like that. I wanted to win. It meant everything to me – not to beat another person but to set myself a personal challenge and meet it in the best way possible. I didn't like to think I was wasting my time.

In randori, I would just think about throwing people. If something didn't work, I would wonder about that. Not until later in my career did I start thinking about why I was thrown in randori or competition – though I must admit that it wasn't very often that happened anyway.

Once I joined the national squad, I started to write down what happened after every training session or every competition – and not just what I was taught. If something slightly unusual happened, I would note it. If I used a slightly different entry or a combination into a favourite throw which worked – or didn't work – I would note it. This was partly to help me remember, because it is extremely easy to have a real insight into a judo technique but simply to forget it; and partly because the writing helped to clarify it in my own mind.

For years, I simply competed. I didn't think of losing weight or putting on weight, I just went in to the appropriate category. It was only when I became involved at international level that I took a more serious view of my training – but even after I won my first world title, I would do slightly crazy things like come back and fight in a team competition a week or so afterwards.

It is impossible to live at this intense level, however. The flamboyant energy of youth will sustain that kind of life for a while, but something will finally say: 'Stop, you have had enough for the moment.'

Because I was so keen I wouldn't listen to other people's advice. Roy Inman used to tell me to stop training – rather an unusual thing for a coach to say to his athlete. But I wouldn't stop. I felt fine, full of beans and raring to go. So I would go out for a run, or find a judo club, or swim or do some weights. Nothing would hold me down.

Then, suddenly, an injury would occur. It may have been a complete accident, like a broken toe or a pulled muscle. But now I tend to feel that often – though not always – it is a sign that it is time to stop. I have had quite a range of injuries in my judo career – pulled ligaments in both knees, broken toes, damaged ligaments in ankles, a bad back for four years, cauliflower ear, and, of course, the broken bones in my foot which means my right foot will always be slightly out of line.

As a result, my obsessive drive to train would be brought to a halt, although if I could train around the injury I would. It took me many knocks and injuries to realise that it was as important to rest after competitions as it was to train. There is a right time to train and a wrong time. Gradually, I started to learn about peaking for the right events and training through others, even though I didn't like the idea of losing at any time.

Preparation Routine

By the time I won my second world title, I was accustomed to a steadier, more sensible training pattern. After all, I wasn't getting any younger. I had cut down dramatically on the events in which I participated. And I established a tapering training programme which I felt gave me the correct amount of time to rest before a major event.

In the week of a competition, I train normally until Tuesday, when I have my last randori session. I continue to do light training – a shortish run, a little bit of uchikomi, more to keep loose and 'have a sweat' than anything else – on Wednesday and Thursday. Friday is normally spent travelling to the competition, in BJA uniform if the event is abroad.

If I am fighting on the Sunday, I spend quite an easy Saturday, with just one 'sweat' session, partly to keep the weight in control and partly to help to dissipate any slight build-up of nerves. I will watch the first day's competition, supporting the British girls. I am basically a loner, and this shows at competitions, where I can often be found sitting by myself or lying on the seats, in a tracksuit, with my earphones on, listening to pop and oblivious to the outside world. But on the day before a fight I will be joking and laughing with the other girls – mainly a sign of nervous tension.

On the evening before my competition day, I like to weigh about 48.2 kilos. I know that this means that in the morning for the weigh-in I will be about 47.7 – just about right. On the day of the 1987 European Championships in Paris I cut it a bit too fine, weighing in at 47.9 kilos. But I have never been overweight. I tend to get my weight down to 45 kilos and build it up gradually to 48.2 the night before the event.

On the morning of the event, I rise in time for the 6.30 a.m. unofficial weigh-in. I step on the scales and check my weight, wait until the official weigh-in at 7 a.m., and then go and have a good drink. I will have some chocolate (it used to be a bit of a binge, but this is improving as I get older!), and perhaps have a good breakfast before popping back to bed for an hour – not to sleep, just to rest.

All my gear is packed. I want to make sure that I can get to the sports hall with at least time for a good 45-minute warm-up. Even if I am not fighting until midday, I like getting to the stadium early to warm up, and start to feel the competitive atmosphere. By this time, I will know who I have got in the first rounds, but I am never too worried about the draw. I'll take what I get. To be the best you have to beat the best.

I go to the sports hall on the coach with the British team, and go to the warm-up room. I work through a stretching routine methodically, and then move on to uchikomi, some grip fighting and some newaza. Only when I feel quite warm and settled will I stop. This is important to ease mental strain as well as physical tensions.

Most of the morning will be spent in the main hall. I don't really watch the tournament unless there is someone in my weight category whom I haven't seen before. I will watch her, note her major techniques, file the information away in my mind and more or less forget about her. I will retreat into my enclosed world of music and just let my mind wander. I come out of it, however, to support British team members, sometimes calling out and encouraging them. Despite my small frame, people say they can always hear me right across a large sports hall.

About 30 minutes before I am due to fight, I warm up again, this time with a greater sense of urgency. I am told that I look absolutely determined and concentrated, and most of me feels like that. But I do get nervous which I still think is a good sign. When I was young, my parents and friends would come to see me win, but when you become a World Champion people (not family and friends) come to see you get beaten. This is a fact of life – everyone wants to see the man fall off the tightrope. This makes me even more determined, but I am human.

On the Mat

On occasions my legs do feel like jelly when I walk on the mat, and when I take hold at the start. If the pressure has been very bad – and you never know what it is going to be like until you get out there – I can even feel a little dizzy. That is why when I get caught, it tends to be right at the beginning, rather than when I have got into my stride.

And my perceptions during the fight can vary enormously. Sometimes, I am clarity itself: I can see what is happening, what I am doing. I know precisely how the fight is going and can make quite clear judgements about the next thing to do, or what to watch out for. At other times, I go into automatic pilot. I feel what is happening without thinking too clearly. I don't think: 'I will do this now and then that'; instead, the throws and moves just seem to come. The final of the Maastricht World Championships against Fumiko Ezaki of Japan was an example of the first kind, and the final against Loly Verguillas of Spain in the 1986 European Championships in London was an example of the second kind.

Very occasionally, I just can't get going. I feel my timing is all wrong and my fluency is missing. This signals a groundwork day for me, and sometimes it means a loss – as was the case in Strasbourg in 1987 when I lost my first fight against Fabienne Boffin. But this tends to happen during the lesser events.

Recuperation

After the event, I try to get back to the hotel fairly quickly, in order to shower and prepare for the evening celebration. I look forward to these because they are a kind of pressure release valve for me. I can eat and dance and drink and do the kind of things that most people do at least once a weekend, but which strict training routines tend to forbid.

Just how much of a rest I will take after I return to England depends on the importance of the event and the timing of the next one. It may be just a couple of weeks, or it may be as long as two months. I tend to go home to Hull now, rather than stay at my flat in London. I feel comfortable in my family home in Bransholme. Most of my close friends are there and Hull is also further away from the pressures. My London life is usually concerned with training.

However, I have learned that there is no total escape from the pressure of being a World Champion. There are prizes attached to titles, but there are penalties too.

Appendix

My Major Competition Results

1975
AJA Area Championships (under 30 kilos, under 35 kilos): gold
AJA National Championships (under 30 kilos): gold

1976
Hull National Dock Labour Board Club Championships: gold, plus award for best ippon throw
AJA Area Championships (under 35 kilos): gold
National Team Championships, Yorkshire and Humberside: bronze

1977
AJA National Championships (under 35 kilos): gold

1979
BJA Yorkshire Championships (under 52 kilos): gold
Humberside Championships (under 48 kilos), junior and under 21: gold
National Team Championships, Yorkshire and Humberside: gold

1980
Kingston Judo Club Championships: gold
Northern Area Championships: gold
British Open Championships: bronze
Consett Open Northern Area Championships: gold
National Championships (under 48 kilos), under 18: gold
National Team Championships, Yorkshire and Humberside: bronze

1981
British Senior Trials: gold
Scottish Open: gold
North of England: gold
European Championships: gold
Yorkshire and Humberside Championships: silver
British National Championships: silver
Dutch Open Championships: gold
National Team Championships, Yorkshire and Humberside: gold
British Open Championships: gold
Canada Cup: gold

1982
British Trials: gold
West German Open Championships: gold
European Championships: gold
Scottish Open Championships: gold
Northern Open Championships: gold
Humberside Open Championships: gold
Austrian Open Championships: gold
Midland Area Open Championships: gold
Dutch Open Championships: gold
French Open Championships: silver
British Open Championships: gold
World Championships: gold

1983
British Trials: gold
European Championships: gold
British National Championships: gold
Midland Area Championships: gold
Austrian Open Championships: gold
American Open Championships: bronze
Fukuoka Championships: gold

1984
West German Open Championships: silver
European Championships: gold

Swiss Open Championships: gold
Dutch Open Championships: silver (retired injured before final)
British Open Championships: silver
World Championships: gold
British Trials (under 52 kilos): gold
Fukuoka Championships (under 48 kilos): gold

1985
West German Open Championships (under 52 kilos): gold
European Championships (under 52 kilos): bronze
Austrian Open Championships (under 48 kilos): bronze
European Team Championships: bronze
Fukuoka Championships (under 48 kilos): gold

1986
European Championships: gold
Commonwealth Games: gold
Austrian Open Championships: gold
British Open Championships: gold
World Championships: gold
Fukuoka Championships: gold

1987
French Open Championships: bronze
European Championships: gold
British Open Championships: gold

Glossary

Ago-oshi Pushing; chin.
Aiki A form of self-defence, based on special principles (lit. harmony of spirit).
Aikido The 'way' of Aiki.
Aite Opponent, partner.
Arashi Storm (e.g. *yama-arashi*; mountain storm).
Ashiwaza Leg or foot technique.
Atama Head.
Ate Strike, hit, punch or kick.
Atemiwaza Striking techniques using hand, elbow, knee, foot etc.
Bo-jutsu Stick or staff fighting.
Bu Martial or military.
Bushi A knight of feudal Japan.
Chui Penalty (equivalent to five points).
Dan Step. A black-belt holder.
De (v. deru) To come out, to advance (e.g. *De-ashi-barai*).
Do (a) Way, path, etc. This word was frequently used in Chinese and Japanese philosophy in the sense of the way of doing an act in the moral and ethical sphere as well as the physical. Kano 'borrowed' it from these sources.
(b) Trunk of the body.
Dojo Training hall or room in which judo is practised.
Eri Collar, lapel.
Eri-jime Strangulation by use of collar.
Gake (v. kakeru) To hang, hook, block.
Garami (v. garamu) To entangle, wrap, bend.
Gari To reap, as with a scythe.
Gasshuku Judo students lodging together for training.
Gokyo The forty (original) throws in judo.
Gono-sen-no-kata Forms of counter technique.
Go-shin-jutsu The art of self-protection (in all its forms).
Gyaku Reverse, upside-down.
Ha Wing.
Hadaka Naked.
Hajime Start, referee's call to commence a contest.
Hane Spring (e.g. *hane-goshi*; spring hip).
Hansoku-make Loss by disqualification (penalty equivalent to ten points).
Hantei Judgement, the referee's call at the end of a drawn contest, requesting the corner judges to indicate who, in their opinion, was the better of the two contestants.
Hara Stomach.
Harai, harai (v. harau) To clear away, sweep.
Harai-goshi Sweeping loin throw.
Harai-tsuri-komi-ashi Sweeping drawing ankle.
Hidari Left side.
Hiji Elbow (e.g. *hiji-ate*; to hit with the elbow).
Hikki (v. hikku) To pull.
Hikki-waki A draw in contest.
Hiza Knee.
Hiza-guruma Knee wheel.
Hon (a) Basic. (b) Number suffix for counting long cylindrical objects, therefore *ippon-seoi-nage*; one-arm shoulder throw.
Ippon One point (score value of ten points).
Itsutsu-no-kata Forms of five (the five elements/principles).
Jigotai Defensive posture.
Jikan Time (time out).
Jita-kyoei The principle that individual advancement benefits society as a whole.

Joseki The place in a dojo or hall where the seniors or VIPs sit.
Ju (a) Soft gentle. This word is taken from Taoist philosophy and embodies the opposite of hard, extreme, unreasonable. Hence the use of 'ju' in judo does not imply soft (as a synonym of easy), but rather reasonable, efficient. Physical action in judo is not meant to be easy (weak) so much as economic. By using the body to its best advantage and exploiting the weaknesses of the opponent, maximum effect can be obtained with maximum efficiency.
(b) Ten.
Ju jitsu, ju jutsu, jui jitsu A name covering many forms of close combat in Japan.
Judo An Olympic sport, combat, art, derived from the ancient arts of ju jitsu by the founder Jigoro Kano.
Judogi The clothes worn when practising or competing at judo, comprising jacket, trousers and belt.
Judoka A high-grade judo player, but used in the West as a convenient word to describe anybody who practises judo.
Juji-jime Normal cross strangle.
Ju-no-kata The forms of 'gentleness'.
Kaeshi, gaeshi In judo this means 'counter' (e.g. *Osoto-gaeshi*; major outer counter).
Kaeshiwaza Technique of counter throw.
Kai, kwai Society, club.
Kake The point of the throw, the point of maximum power.
Kame (a) Upper, top. (b) Paper. (c) God(s).
Kani-basami 'Scissors' throw.
Kansetsu A joint (of the body).
Kansetsuwaza A joint technique. (Note: in a judo contest only elbow locks are permitted, but this term can be used to describe a lock on any joint.)
Kao Face.
Karate Literally 'empty-handed'; a system of fighting without weapons, striking the hands, feet, elbows, etc.
Kata (a) Form. A training method used in judo and most martial arts, a drill. (b) One of a pair. (c) Shoulder (e.g. *kata-guruma*; shoulder wheel).
Kata-guruma Shoulder wheel.
Kata-ha-jime Shoulder wing choke-lock.
Kata-juji-jime Half-cross strangle.
Katame, gatame (v. katemeru) To harden.
Katamewaza Groundwork technique.
Katsu, kappo Methods of resuscitation.
Keiko Practice.
Keikoku Severe penalty (equivalent to seven points).
Kempo A method of fighting founded in Shorinji similar to ju jitsu.
Ken Sword.
Kendo The 'way' of the sword (Japanese two-handed fencing).
Kesa A Buddhist monk's surplice, worn diagonally across the body. Thus there is the technique known as *kesa-gatame*, but which in free translation into English is referred to as scarf hold.
Ki Psychic energy said to be centred in the *saikatanden*.
Kiai A shout used to harden the body and strengthen the will when maximum effort is required.
Kime (v. kakeru) To decide.
Kime-no-kata Forms of decision, which are the kata of self-protection.
Kiri (v. kiru) To cut, as with a knife.
Ko (a) Small, minor (e.g. *kouchi-gari*; minor inner reap). (b) Old, ancient.
Kodokan The headquarters of judo in Japan (Tokyo); the founder's dojo.
Koka A score, almost a yuko (score value of three points).
Koshi, goshi Hips (e.g. koshiwaza; hip techniques).
Koshi-guruma Hip wheel.
Koshiki-no-kata The kata of ancient forms with techniques suitable for people in armour.

Kosoto-gake Minor outside hook.
Kosoto-gari Minor outside reap.
Kouchi-gari Minor inner reap.
Kubi Neck.
Kumikata The method of grappling of two contestants.
Kuruka, guruma (a) Wheel (e.g. *oguruma;* major wheel). (b) Vehicle.
Kuzure (v. kuzureru) To crumble, collapse, break down. Thus a free translation of *Kuzure-kesa-gatame* would be broken scarf hold. A hold that is not quite the basic or pure form (hon).
Kuzure-kame-shiho-gatame Broken upper four quarters.
Kuzushi The balance broken.
Kyu A judo 'student' grade.
Ma Direct, exact, absolutely (e.g. Masutemiwaza; direct sacrifice throw to the rear).
Machi-dojo Street dojo, small local dojo.
Mae Front.
Makikomi Winding, to wrap or roll up, to throw by rolling oneself so that the opponent is 'locked on' to one's body.
Ma-sutemi-waza Technique whereby the performer (tori) falls straight on to his back to throw.
Mata The thigh.
Matte Refereeing word meaning 'wait'.
Migi Right side.
Mizu Water.
Mon Gate, junior grade.
Morote Both hands (e.g. *morote-seoi-nage;* two-handed shoulder throw).
Morote-gari Two-handed throw by clasping opponent's legs.
Mune Chest (e.g. *mune-gatame;* chest hold).
Nage (v. nageru) To throw (e.g. nagewaza; throwing techniques).
Nage-no-kata The forms of throwing, fifteen selected throws executed both left and right to train the participants in body control and appreciation of judo technique.
Name Wave (of water).
Nami In a line, in a row.
Ne (v. neru) To lie down.
Newaza Technique carried out in a lying-down position.
No Belonging to. A link word as in *nage-no-kata*.
O Big, large, major (e.g. *ouchi-gari;* major inner reaping).
Obi Belt.
Ogoshi Major hip technique.
Oguruma Major wheel.
Okuri (v. okuru) To send forward.
Okuri-ashi-barai Sweeping ankle throw.
Okuri-eri-jime Sliding collar strangle.
Osaekomi Holding (e.g. osaekomi-waza; holding techniques); referee's call signalling that a hold is effective.
Oshi (v. osu) To push.
Osoto-gari Major outer reaping.
Osoto-otoshi Major outer drop.
Otoshi (v. otosu) To drop.
Ouchi-gari Major inner reaping.
Ouchimata Major or great inner thigh.
Randori Free practice.
Rei Bow.
Renraku Connection, communication, contact.
Renrakuwaza Combination technique.
Renshu Free practice or exercise.
Renzokuwaza Comprehensive name for techniques linked up in any way.
Ronin An unretained samurai warrior.
Ryote Two hands.
Ryu Method or style. Attached to most of the names of the old ju jitsu systems (e.g. Kito Ryu).
Samurai A knight of feudal Japan (a social class).
Sasae To support, prop (e.g. *sasae-tsuri-komi-ashi;* propping drawing ankle).
Sei-ryoku-senyo The principle of maximum efficiency in the use of mind and body.
Sensei Teacher, Master (or person of high standing).
Senshu A competitor, champion.

Seoi (v. seou) To carry on the back (translated into English, *seoi-nage* is more commonly known as 'shoulder throw').
Seoi-otoshi Shoulder drop.
Seppuku The Bushi method of committing suicide. Normally erroneously called hara-kiri.
Shikai Contest.
Shido Note (penalty equivalent to three points).
Shihan Master, past-master.
Shiho Four quarters, four directions.
Shiki Style, ceremony.
Shime, jime (v. shimeru) To tighten, strangle.
Shimewaza Technique of strangling.
Shizentai Natural (upright) posture.
Sode Sleeve.
Sode-tsuri-komi-goshi Sleeve resisting hip throw.
Sogo-gachi Compound win by ippon made up of a score of waza-ari added to the benefit of a keikoku penalty.
Sono-mama Freeze, do not move (referee's instruction to the two combatants in a contest when he requires them to stay absolutely still).
Sore-made That is all, finish (referee's command terminating the contest).
Soto Outside, outer (e.g. *osoto-gari*; major outer reap).
Sukui (v. sukuu) To scoop up.
Sumi Corner.
Sutemi (v. suteru) To throw away.
Sutemiwaza Technique whereby the attacker sacrifices his own posture.
Tachi (v. tatsu) To stand.
Tachi-rei Standing bow.
Tachiwaza Technique performed in the standing position.
Tai Body.
Tai-sabaki Body movement.
Tani Valley (e.g. *tani-otoshi*; valley drop).
Tatami Rice straw mats used in dojos and Japanese houses.
Tate Vertical.
Te Hand (e.g. tewaza; hand techniques).
Tekubi Wrist.
Toketa Hold broken. A command given by the referee to indicate to the timekeeper that the 'count must stop' when a contestant has effectively broken the hold by which he was being secured.
Tokui Favourite, special (e.g. tokui waza; favourite technique).
Tomoe Turning over, twisting over, whirling over. It is difficult to find the exact translation in English, but *tomoe-nage* freely translated is commonly known in English as stomach throw.
Tori (v. toru) (a) The name used often in technical explanation for the person who applies the technique. (b) To grasp, to hold in the hands.
Tsugi-ashi A manner of walking in which one foot leads at each step and the other never passes it.
Tsukiwaza Poke, stab, thrust or punch technique.
Tsukuri (v. tsukuru) The action of breaking the opponent's balance.
Tsuri To 'fish' up (e.g. *tsuri-komi*; lift up and pull forward).
Tsuri-komi-goshi Resisting hip throw.
Uchikomi (v. utsukomu) To beat against, go in. A repetitive exercise where the throwing technique is taken to the point of kake.
Uchimata Inner thigh.
Ude Arm.
Ude-garami Arm entanglement.
Ue Above, on top of.
Uke (v. ukeru) To receive. The name often used in technical explanations for the person on whom the technique is applied.
Ukemi The 'breakfall'.
Uki (v. uku) To float, buoyant.
Uki-goshi Floating hip.
Ura Back, rear (e.g. *uranage*; rear throw).
Ushiro Behind, back of (e.g. *ushiro-jime*; any strangle from behind).
Utsuri (v. utsuru) To change, to move (e.g. *Utsuri-goshi*; changing hip).

Wakare (v. wakareru) To divide, separate (e.g. *yoko-wakare*; side separation).
Waki Armpit.
Waza Technique.
Waza-ari A score, almost an ippon (score value of seven points).
Waza-ari awesete ippon Ippon achieved by having scored two waza-ari.
Yama Mountain.
Yoko Side (e.g. *yoko-shiho-gatame;* side four quarters).
Yoko-sutemiwaza Side sacrifice throw.
Yoshi Let's go, let's get on with it. Referee's instruction used after sono-mama to resume the contest.
Yuko A score, almost waza-ari (score value of five points).
Yusei-gachi A win by superiority.
Za-rei Formal kneeling bow or salutation.
Za-zen Kneeling motionless in concentrated thought, meditation.
Zori Toe-grip straw sandals used by judoka when in judogi moving to and from the mat edge.

Index